THRIVE

AND

SURVIVE,

Zero to Five

2 SISTERS, 14 CHILDREN, AND WHAT WE WISH WE'D KNOWN FROM THE BEGINNING

THRIVE
AND
SURVIVE,
Zero to Five

2 SISTERS, 14 CHILDREN, AND
WHAT WE WISH WE'D KNOWN
FROM THE BEGINNING

MARGARET JOHNSON NYMAN
and MARY JOHNSON PETERSON

REDEMPTION
PRESS

ISBN 13: 978-1-68314-879-1
ePub ISBN: 978-1-68314-880-7
Kindle ISBN: 978-1-68314-881-4
Library of Congress Catalog Card Number: 2019934499

To our 7 plus 7.

A Tribute

Without my sister Mary's influence on this book, it would never have come to be. She brought structure to the ideas, and only after her work was done, could I attach the details. As always, I simply followed her lead. About halfway through, we learned Mary had terminal cancer, a terrible blow to both of us. We shelved our project and waited to see what God would do. Happily, He led us back to the book. Our sister-time lasted only two and a half years after that, but thanks to Mary's resolve, we finished our project. I'm thankful we can still hear her wise voice in these pages.

Margaret

Table of Contents

INTRODUCTION

The two of us were sharing tuna sandwiches at the kitchen table one day when hilarious toddler laughter floated into the room. Rushing to a nearby bathroom, we found two of our children, one-year-old Klaus and two-year-old Andrew, finishing a series of flushes. A bowlful of toilet paper swirled just beneath the rim, and our boys were patting and poking the mush with their hands.

Unrolling four rolls had been a good time, but turning it into toidy stew had been even better. When they finally noticed us, their big grins said, "Isn't this great?"

Grandpa had been right when he tagged young children as little scientists. "Don't punish them for wanting to learn how things work," he said. Never mind that this particular science project included a professional plumber and a hefty bill.

Both of us have loved being moms for the last forty-five years, but like all mothers, much of what we've experienced has been a surprise. The phrase *guesswork mothering* applies. For example, no one told us that as moms we'd have to do radical things like hold down a silky-skinned baby while a doctor punctured him with a needle. And who knew we'd spend ten minutes working to get a one-second smile from a newborn?

Much of motherhood followed no logic as we were yanked through one unexpected situation after another. And when we finally got each bout of confusion sorted, that bit was over but a new one had begun.

So what's a mommy to do? If we could start over with the accumulated understanding of our mothering years, we would do in our own families the things you'll find in this book. For starters, we'd store the toilet paper on a high shelf.

God often uses the foolish (children) to confound the wise (parents). Of course, being confounded (think perplexed) is usually unpleasant. It does, however, mobilize us to get counsel from someone who's been where we're going.

We hope these pages offer encouragement to you in your high calling as a mom. Since God equips those He calls rather than calling the already equipped, think of this book as one piece of equipment in your parenting tool kit. We've raised fourteen children between us, seven apiece, not one of whom came with a warning label. Since the world is quick to acknowledge mothering as a difficult job, without directions, who can succeed?

This book is the instruction manual we wish we'd had back at the beginning— the would-haves, should-haves, and could-haves of mothering. We're a couple of older moms wanting to share what worked and what didn't. Names have not been changed to protect the innocent, because none of our kids are innocent.

And good for you for wanting to be the best mom you can be. If you're feeling overwhelmed, please know you're not alone. Can you hear us cheering you on?

Mary and Margaret

Chapter 1

CONSIDER THE END
BEFORE YOU BEGIN

Let us not become weary in doing good,
for at the proper time we will reap a harvest if we do not give up.
Galatians 6:9

What's every mom's worst nightmare? Losing one of her kids. In ten minutes, I (Margaret) lost two.

Wrestling five children into winter wear for a trip to the local park district had exhausted me, and we weren't even in the car yet. As I readied the last, the first was pulling off his coat. "I'm hot," he said.

This would be my first outing since baby number five's birth, managing all of them by myself. Little Hans was only three weeks old. "Help me, Lord," I said, while strapping seventeen-month-old Klaus into his car seat.

Once at the park's office, I busied myself filling out paperwork for four-year-old Linnea's gymnastics class, proud of myself for remembering the checkbook. Suddenly I went cold. "Where's the new baby?" I asked, still not used to using his name.

The children stopped roughhousing and looked on the floor as if I might have set him down there. "Is he in the car?" I said, alarms going off in my head.

I ran for the double doors, forgetting my checkbook on the counter. The children followed. Finding the infant car seat empty, I panicked. "Everybody into the car!"

Without buckling up, we flew out of the parking lot toward home. Where was the baby? How could I be so irresponsible! God, help me.

Squealing into the driveway, I left the car running and bolted into the house, eyes darting from side to side in search of my newborn. "Hans!" (Of course he couldn't answer.) Where had I put him? The front hall was empty. Living room too. "Hans!" When had I last seen him? How long ago had I touched him? It was zipping up his snowsuit. Our bedroom.

And sure enough, there he was, sound asleep in the middle of the bed right where I'd left him, unaware of the crisis swirling around him. With hands shaking, I picked him up and hugged him to my chest, my throat burning. "Thank you, God!"

The older children rushed into the room, relieved to see their new brother intact and their mommy back to normal. Scanning the lineup, I asked, "Where's Klaus?"

Remembering that I'd left the engine running and seat belts unbuckled, I stiffened with fear for my toddler. "Is he in the car?" I pushed past the children toward the front door.

"No," said Linnea. "He's not here."

"What do you mean?"

"He's by my gymnastics class."

"Back in the car!"

Sweat trickled from my underarms as we raced back to the office, this time with Hans. Sure enough, Linnea was right. There was my toddler, sitting on the high counter next to my checkbook, encircled by the arms of the park district secretary.

"I knew you'd be back," she said with a broad grin.

"Oh, God," I said out loud. "Please help me."

***

Motherhood is exhausting. On a bad day, it swamps us. Every mom experiences chaos now and then as she does the most important job on earth because each of us is only one person with two arms. We can't do it all perfectly. You may never have five children, but each one is a full-time job you're trying to squeeze into a life that's already full.

Even though I'd had a chunk of mothering experience by the time Hans arrived, I was inexperienced at managing life with *this* baby and the new logistical challenges he brought. Though trying my best that day at the park district, I chalked up a big, fat failure. How do we moms avoid the pitfalls of poor parenting when so much of what we do is trial and error, or better said, trying with errors?

Back then, when we would ask an older mother what to do in a new set of circumstances, she'd say, "Oh, I'm not qualified to give you any advice. I made too many mistakes."

That's precisely why she could have shared with credibility, describing what she might do differently if she could start again. She could have said, "I can tell you what worked for me and what didn't. Together we can come up with a way to handle your situation." What an encouragement that would have been for us as new moms, flooded with questions and deficient in self-confidence.

One biblical mandate is that older women teach younger ones whatever God has taught them. Despite mistakes, the experienced mothers we knew had a wealth of knowledge they could have shared. Now, after four decades of mothering, we see how we actually learned more through failure than success.

We wish someone had told us that losing track of children—or any other parenting failure—doesn't brand a woman as a bad mother. You might experience one incident of poor mothering, but you're not doomed to permanent failure because of it. The many tears I shed after I messed up at the park district office could have been avoided had someone with experience let me know these things happen despite our best efforts. Raising a child takes a long time and is the composite of thousands of experiences. That afternoon was just one.

MARATHON OR SPRINT: WHAT DIFFERENCE DOES PERSEVERANCE MAKE?

I (Mary) remember going into labor with my seventh child, Marta, after a jam-packed day with the others, and I had steady contractions through the night. As the baby arrived early in the morning, I viewed my little daughter through the lens of exhaustion. The nurse handed her to me while I was still on the delivery table, which flooded me with fresh awareness of the long journey ahead: sleep deprivation, isolation, less time with my husband, the day-and-night demands of a newborn, and further depletion of what little energy I had left.

At that moment I wasn't sure I could make it, and I felt reluctant to even take the baby into my arms. But mothering is a marathon, not a sprint. We don't have to do it all the first week, month, or year. There will be times of rest and refreshment along the way, just as marathon runners accept cups of cool water and encouraging words while they run.

I (Margaret) recall gazing down at my own sleeping newborn when he was only hours old. He was the one who first ushered me into motherhood. "Look at this sweet little guy, so angelic." I said. "How hard could it be?"

By the middle of the first night at home, when his crying wouldn't stop, I got my answer: it would be the hardest thing I ever did. When my mother arrived the next morning to do dishes and sweep floors, the greater gift was in her words.

Gathering my crying baby into her lap, she spoke directly into his pinched face. "Nelson, you are the best thing that ever happened to your mommy. Oh, the joy she will have for the rest of her life because of you."

The rest of my life? It hadn't dawned on me I would be a mother that long. Once I recovered from the shock, I connected with the truth of marathon mothering in a way that affected everything I did from then on. My mom had given me a perspective I badly needed as a twentysomething who'd been a mother for five days.

The fact that our baby's first twelve hours at home were full of misery and tears (both his and mine) didn't mean it would always be that way. Today was a new day, tomorrow another. We would have many months and years together as mother and son. This realization took the pressure off the moments filled with crying. Better days were coming.

It's also comforting to know that mothers don't have to rush in loving, influencing, and serving their children. The flip side, though, is that it can be exasperating never being able to see the finish line. Every mother has to figure out what to do with that reality.

Twenty-one years of mothering amounts to 8,760 hours. We're in a marathon, not a sprint, parenting one hour at a time. Once we stop straining to figure out when our running will end, we can calm down enough to enjoy (or deal with) the moment. We can manage the race like a distance runner, not bolting at top speed unnecessarily but setting a comfortable pace for the long haul. Steady perseverance will get both mom and child where they want to go.

The Bible speaks about this in Isaiah 28:10 KJV: "For precept must be upon precept, precept upon precept; line upon line, line upon line; here a little, and there a little." We don't think there's any other place in the Bible where an instruction is double repeated like that. As a matter of fact, this advice is so important that the Lord repeats it three verses later in exactly the same way, amounting to a quadruple impact.

Isn't this a great description of mothering? A precept is only one statement; a line smaller yet; a little bit here, a little more there. That's what mothers are called to do, and by the time children reach adulthood, much has been written on their hearts and accomplished in their lives.

Know this from the beginning, however: even though children grow up, mothering doesn't end. When your newborn is placed in your arms, her whole world is you. As the old proverb says, "To the world you might be one person, but to one person, you are the world."

As you move through the days and gradually the years with that child, the relationship will change. While her life broadens, you'll become a smaller part of her world and be only one of many influencers. Even in the distant future, though, when one day you're on your deathbed, you'll continue to be her mother, hopefully still taking advantage of the chance to put precept upon precept, line upon line.

Our mother modeled this principle with excellence. She was teaching right up to her last breath, pointing us to what was most important to her. On her deathbed, she was aware of the powerful teaching moment at hand and used it to full advantage.

I (Mary) was sitting with Mom shortly before she died, whispering a favorite Bible passage into her ear (a passage she'd paid us to memorize as children, at five cents a verse). Although she was too weak to even lift her arm off the bed, as I recited John 14, Mom's dreamy expression confirmed her trust in its message about heaven. Though she didn't have the energy to speak every line, she was able to fill in the blanks when I paused at important words. In a raspy whisper, she got them right.

"Let not your heart be . . ." And she filled in *troubled.*

"Ye believe in . . . *God,* believe also in . . . *me.* In my Father's house are many . . . *mansions.*"

When I got to the next line, "If it were not so, I would have told . . ." she didn't respond with the word *you.* So the last word my mother spoke was *mansions,* and she died shortly thereafter. Even in death, she was still running the mothering marathon, modeling one last precept: when everything else had been stripped away, God and His Word were all she had, but they were enough.

Seeds or Weeds, What Will Your Harvest Be?

Picture a farmer standing at the edge of an acre of dirt, contemplating the task ahead. Let's say it's an old-fashioned farmer from a hundred years ago. Without automated equipment, he knows planting his wheat will be a long-term, backbreaking job.

He stands and thinks, *How many holes will I have to dig? How many times will I have to bend over to plant, cover, and pat down seeds?*

How does he motivate himself to get started with that first hole and seed? It can only be the vision of that same field full of tall, waving wheat ready for harvest.

Just as a farmer might feel swamped with the enormity of his task, you as a mother might feel overwhelmed too. Combat this by thinking of the adult your little one will one day become. The farmer could easily bend over and plant one seed. Today you are able to do one task, teach one precept, or say one line that benefits your child. Focus not on the length of the assignment but on the delight of the end product. Then one at a time, plant your seeds.

The laws of sowing and reaping apply beautifully to parenting.

Law #1: You reap what you sow. If you plant an acorn, you get an oak tree yielding acorns, not chestnuts. If you look children in the eyes when you talk to them, they'll eventually do the same to you and others. If you demand honesty from them, in the end they'll be honest adults.

Law #2: You reap in a different season than you sow.
As you sow good things into your children, the produce from
your efforts will come . . . but later. You might have to "assist"
a youngster to put his dirty clothes in the hamper twenty times
before he'll do it on his own. You might have to demonstrate
patience a thousand times before she follows whatever example
you've set. But eventually your faithfulness to plant will reap a
harvest.

As the farmer of long ago sowed each seed, he had to bury
it. It was hidden for a while, and he knew he wouldn't see the
first signs of growth as they occurred beneath the sod. Similarly,
we won't see a growth in maturity in our children until time
has passed.

Law #3: You reap more than you sow. This can be both
frightening and encouraging when we realize thousands of
acorns come from one oak tree. If you sow something negative
into the life of your child, you'll get it back in multiples of bad.
But the opposite is also true. Planting good habits, good words,
good character traits will result in multiples of good.

If you want your child to show tenderness in his future
relationships, you must handle him with gentleness today.
If you hope he'll be a patient adult, you must respond with
calm control now, even when he's on a crying jag. Once you
have the harvest in mind, planting small seeds takes on more
importance.

In another example, if you want your child to become a
financially responsible person one day, you can get her started

while she's still a toddler. Label empty jars with three colors and three words: *saving* in blue, *giving* in green, and *spending* in red. Let your little one make penny deposits regularly. Seeing coins accumulate in the savings jar lays the groundwork for fiscal responsibility later.

Dropping coins from the giving jar into the Sunday school offering teaches generosity. And spending her own pennies to buy a toy teaches the value of money and the joy of saving long enough to get something valuable. It's also true that when she empties her own spending jar at the store, she's bound to take better care of what she buys.

It took us years to realize we were planting seeds in our children every minute we were with them. But there were also seeds being planted when we weren't there by what was hanging on their bedroom walls, by who we invited into our homes, by how we spoke to their daddies. When a critical spirit popped up in one of the children, we realized with great pain that it was probably because we'd planted a bad seed without even knowing it.

When we see something negative coming out of our youngsters, before we come down too hard on them, we should ask ourselves, "Did I contribute to this?" Consider the end before you begin. It's easier to be careful when planting seeds than to get rid of bad seeds/weeds after they've put stubborn roots deep into your children.

Maybe your goal is to raise a grateful child, one who will say thank you and recognize blessings every day. You begin by prompting him to say thanks when others show kindness to him. Even more important, practice your own attitude of gratitude in front of him. As he grows, make a habit of pointing out blessings. "Look at that pretty flower. Aren't you glad God made it like that?" or "Your friend's skin is a different color than yours. Didn't God make people in lots of interesting ways?"

If you think about the distant seasons in a child's life, the goals you've set in the early days will always be on your mind, creating the precepts and lines that come from your mouth.

LAWS OF SOWING AND REAPING

1. You reap what you sow. (Plant corn; reap corn.)
2. You reap in a different season than you sow. (Plant in spring; harvest in fall.)
3. You reap more than you sow. (One seed yields hundreds more.)

So what are the most important planting times in every child's day? There are two, when the soil of his heart is most fertile and ready for your good seeds: first thing in the morning and the last thing at night.

Be careful how you greet your little one when you first see him each day. Do you smile? Do you reach eagerly for him? Do you share words of optimism and joy? Do you communicate blessings? The garden of a young heart is ready for planting right then. Be sure not to waste this rich opportunity.

I (Margaret) remember failing miserably at this in the early years of my mothering. With three preschoolers, I found it nearly impossible to have any effective quiet time with the Lord. Nowhere in my day was there a pocket of peace with my name on it. Every time I sat down with my Bible or prayer list, a baby would cry, a glass of milk would go over, or a skirmish would erupt.

The only way to get a few minutes was to set my alarm for 5:00 a.m. and beat the rush. Though I found intermittent success this way, I was often frustrated when one of the children would wake "ahead of schedule" and steal my precious few minutes.

How well I recall the morning I got an "F" in mothering. Still in my pajamas, I had gathered my Bible, notebook, pen, and mug of coffee. Tiptoeing past the stairs toward the living room, eager to eat a spiritual breakfast, I glanced up to see our toddler sitting on the top step . . . already! When he saw me come around the corner, his face lit up, and he greeted me in his usual cheery fashion. "Mama!"

In a split second my face fell, going from neutral to angry, exactly as our eyes met. Thinking only of myself, I let out a low moan. This child had robbed me of something valuable. My treasure had been blown out of the room by the cold wind of an interruption I was having trouble accepting. And there the two of us froze, a chasm of disconnect between us.

"Why are you out of bed so early?" I said with irritation, knowing this was a question no toddler could answer. Still caught up with my own agenda, it took a minute for my displeasure to calm. I turned toward the kitchen to put away my Bible, notebook, and pen, while my little guy bounced down the steps on his bottom, eager to put his arms around me.

Thankfully God convicted me quickly, and we made up in a hurry. I tried to backpedal my poor performance, but I felt bad then and still do today, more than forty years later. But motherhood doesn't come with do-overs. I squandered the chance to plant a good seed and planted a weed instead.

Weed Wisdom

- Weeds are a fact of life.
- Pull weeds while they're still small.
- Weeds are stronger than tender plants.
- Don't mistake weeds for good plants.
- Unpulled weeds will destroy a garden.

I learned a valuable lesson that day. I could aim for an early-morning quiet time with the Lord, but if a child interrupted me, I knew it was that same Lord's first choice for me to set my Bible aside and deliver a happy greeting and a warm hug. Planting must come before harvesting.

Your initial connection with a child in the morning is one optimal planting time, and the other is at bedtime. No young child wants to go to bed. It means separation from parents and isolation from anything else going on in the house.

Most children will stall as long as possible. Why not take advantage of those moments together to plant some good seeds? When you're encircled by the intimate glow of a night-light and snuggled close with a child who's enjoying your company, warm communication comes easily.

With very little children, you can sing a quiet song. Toddlers love a board book or two. Preschool kids like to talk. A prayer of thanks and blessing is appropriate for all ages.

Several of our fourteen children have prayed to receive Jesus into their lives during these important planting times at the close of a day. The soil of their hearts received seeds of biblical wisdom as they asked countless questions about life and truth. Bedtime can also be the perfect time to memorize Scripture in small bites, placing God's powerful Word into their minds as the last thought of the day.

Although I (Mary) knew it was important to close each day on a positive note, some days were so stressful I could hardly wait to end them. The promise of starting fresh the next morning sounded better than trying to bring contentment into the moment. But my regular bedtime goal was to spend one-on-one quiet time with each young child after his bath as he settled down for sleep.

This routine for the little ones meant lap time in my antique rocker. I look at that rocker today and cherish the memories associated with it. (It was given to me by my own mother, who was rocked in it by her mother.) I remember nursing newborns and cuddling with toddlers like little Andrew, who contentedly took his last bottle of the day while twirling my hair between his pudgy fingers.

On the good days, when I wasn't completely spent by bedtime, I'd let the child choose several favorite books, after I had "stacked the deck" with stories that were both short and sweet. These had few words and few pages, making them a quick read. And none of them mentioned sharks, monsters, or wild storms. Thirty years later, I still have the words memorized to Karl's favorite, *The Little Engine That Could*, and Marta's favorite, *Harry the Dirty Dog*.

Consider the value of those few bedtime minutes in the lives of young children. If I can remember the words to those books decades later, so can they. Give careful thought to what you read to them, not just for the enjoyment of that moment, but also the impact on their futures.

Even when I was tempted to jump over our reading routine, I knew deep down it was an important seed-planting time. The question is, did I make the most of it?

Would the fruit have looked different or would there have been more fruit had I incorporated additional biblical wisdom into this nighttime reading? Could I have concentrated on hiding God's Word as well as the can-do attitude of the little blue engine into those young hearts? Decide what you want to communicate to your child and then zero in on those things.

After tucking them into bed, I would pray with each child, focusing on thankfulness. To establish good habits when they're younger than you think they can understand is good training for you and assists them in sliding into an established routine. Sadly, I didn't pray with my newborns because I was often longing just to get that baby to sleep. Some of them needed a thousand gentle pats to go into dreamland. (Yes, while hanging over the crib. I actually counted.) Often our bedtime rituals were inconvenient for me and sometimes even a burden. If you feel the same, don't give up. It's important, and there are no do-overs.

Seed Savvy

- Good seeds need nourishing soil.
- Seedlings are fragile and need shelter.
- Young plants need water and sunshine.
- Plants need cultivating and fertilizing.

Every mom has times when the closing of her child's door at bedtime is the highlight of her day. But as you're able, choose to plant seeds while the soil is warm and soft. Your harvest will be abundant because the Bible says it will: "A man [or woman] reaps what [s]he sows" (Galatians 6:7).

We all know mothers don't get a second crack at raising their kids. Be encouraged to realize every bit of time you do spend, no matter how brief, will bring forth a harvest. Consider the end before you begin. Define the importance of what you're doing while your children are still young, and take advantage of those peak seed-planting times for a future harvest.

When you fail now and then, as we all do, remember that the life lessons with greatest impact are the ones learned by the hardest (and sometimes most regrettable) experiences. Though I (Margaret) lost track of two children that day at the park district, my lesson from failure was learned well. In the twenty-five years of active mothering that followed (including two additional children), I never lost another one.

The one who sows righteousness reaps a sure reward.
Proverbs 11:18

What can you do today?
Hug your child when he least expects it.

We wish we'd known . . .
1. we were farmers.
2. to be intentional about planting good seeds.
3. to weed our gardens faithfully.
4. to anticipate a bountiful harvest.

Chapter 2

THESE ARE THE
BEST YEARS?

Whatever you do, work at it with all your heart . . .
It is the Lord Christ you are serving.
Colossians 3:23–24

My daughter Louisa (Margaret's) came running to me
one spring afternoon when she was three years old. "Mommy!
Mommy!" she said, struggling to keep her hands behind her
back as she ran. "A surprise!"

Stopping in front of me, she brought her closed fists around
and opened them, exposing a dozen crushed daffodil blossoms.
"Look!" she said, with great joy. "For you!"

My first thought was, *You've demolished our entire daffodil crop, and we won't see it again for another year . . .* but I managed to hold my tongue and come out with something positive.

"Uh . . . oh my. They're . . . very pretty." Choking back the lecture I felt like delivering, I said, "Thank you, Weezi. We'll use them on the dinner table tonight."

She skipped off, proud of herself for making her mama happy. It was a good thing she couldn't see inside my head.

As I thought about it later, her daffodil harvesting did have some logic behind it. The day before, we'd made a "daisy chain" of dandelions, and I'd encouraged her to pick them all. "There's one over there! Run and get it! And look, there's another over here!" In her mind, dandelions and daffodils were the same thing. I'd encouraged her to pick one, so why not the other?

Appreciating the Now

Maybe you've heard the old saying, "These are the best years of your life." It's a favorite of older women watching younger moms coping with young children. Both of us heard this from complete strangers and also from older women we knew well, including our own mother. And these women all had one thing in common: their children were grown. Was it a case of rose-colored glasses? Maybe a memory lapse? An expression of wishful thinking?

As you struggle with a fussy baby and a tired toddler, hearing someone say that this is as good as it gets can be demoralizing. But tucked into that older-lady statement is a nugget of motherhood wisdom.

Your children pass through infancy, toddlerhood, and the preschool years assuming you will serve their interests every day and many nights. Because they are, indeed, genuinely needy, you do what has to be done for their welfare, knowing that whether they live or die is really up to you, starting with breastfeeding your newborn on day one. But when you think about it, it's incredibly lopsided. You give, and they take, and then they take some more. Your energy gets depleted while theirs increases. So how can these intense years possibly be the best ones?

What are older ladies actually saying by making that statement? And how can you avoid being pulled down by it?

We believe the best-years remark is more a commentary on getting older and the losses aging brings than a summary of your present-day life. It's never meant to discourage you. Women in middle or old age watch you dealing with your adorable toddler, and they flash back to the eager hugs and sloppy kisses of their own little children. They remember the joy on the face of a three-year-old bringing a scribbled drawing to them, her only intention to make mama happy. And they think back to the pleasure of a two-year-old who finally mastered putting a chunky bead on a shoelace.

This same older lady might also recall that when her youngsters were little, she could do no wrong in their eyes. Young children put their mommies on a pedestal, seeing them as the source of ultimate truth—someone who has their confusing world all figured out. They believe she has the power to keep them safe when they feel threatened by new experiences or people, and they take their behavioral cues from her. In other words, she is the image of God to them, which can be a heavy burden to an already-burdened mommy. But it does come with a few perks.

You have the power to manage and control where your children go, who they spend time with, what they wear, what they eat, and what the hour-to-hour schedule will be. An older mother commenting that these are your best years has traveled many miles away from that position, learning from experience how her influence over her children became less and less. She longs for that time when she was able to provide for them, protect them, and love them in ways they eagerly received.

There's another reason why an older woman admires your stage in life. She recalls what it was like to have a youthful, passionate love for her husband and he for her as they shared the task of raising their children before outside influences interfered. She misses the pitter-patter of a one-year-old's feet and the babyish vocabulary of a two-year-old. She may not have heard a young child's laugh or even a cry for many years, and now both are music to her ears.

And she wishes she could go back.

But that's not all. She looks at your youthful body, your smooth skin, your healthy hair, your strong back, your flexibility, and she mourns her own losses of the same. Time has snatched these things from her, and she knows it's only going to get worse.

So what's the nugget of motherhood wisdom behind her comment that these are your best years? She's simply saying, "Despite your exhaustion and the all-consuming nature of your job, be intentional about noticing and appreciating the now. Don't let this abundance of blessings slip away without acknowledging them, because one day they'll be gone."

COUNT YOUR PHYSICAL BLESSINGS

- Good health
- High energy
- Ache-free joints
- Sharp mind
- Agility
- Active love life
- Toned skin
- Strong arms
- Healthy hair
- Limber back

When your job as a mom overwhelms you and you find yourself longing for your children to hurry and grow up, remember that one day you may look back on these wearisome, jam-packed years and say, "They were indeed good years . . . maybe even the best."

PLANNING TO SUCCEED

I (Margaret) recall a morning when our oldest three children were off at school and the younger two, Klaus and Hans, were ages two and one. After driving the carpool, I was having trouble tackling the breakfast dishes because two little boys were tugging on my legs, whining in discontent, and making me miserable. I felt like a tree they were trying to climb.

I'd done my best to distract them. "Look over there, Hans. Isn't that your favorite truck? *Rrrum-rrrum!*"

"Klaus, would you like an ice cube to play with? Here, have a whole bowl of them!"

But nothing worked. I don't know what possessed me, but I decided to get down on their level to see what they were seeing. On the floor I knee-walked the length of the kitchen counter and back to the sink area, looking up. The problem was evident. My toddlers were trying to climb me simply because they couldn't see what I was doing.

As they watched from below, they saw my arms moving and heard water flowing, but everything else was out of their line of vision. All toddlers long to participate in the activity at hand, so their low vantage point produced great frustration.

Just to see if I'd been right, I put Klaus on a kitchen chair near the sink and plopped Hans atop the counter. Once they could see, the whining stopped, and both boys bubbled over with good cheer.

Of course no mommy can do this every time she does the dishes. But one way to succeed at mothering is to slow your pace to match your children's. Maybe here and there in your busy life you can screech to an almost halt and view life through their eyes. If you do, it'll increase your willingness to include them in your work as it adds to your storehouse of patience. My brief knee-walk gave me a valuable perspective on toddlerhood that I haven't forgotten. Letting two little boys see what their mommy was doing put all three of us into the same slow moment. The boys appreciated it, and thirty years later, I'm still smiling at the memory.

During these years when you're consumed with caring for young children, your job will be less difficult if you're able to slow down. It'll reduce stress all around and bring a greater measure of parenting success. Practice being in the moment rather than thinking, *If only he would leave me alone so I could get my work done.*

Once we go down that road, the if-onlys never end: *If only she would start walking, I'd feel less like a packhorse. If only I could get him toilet trained, life would be easier.* Following this pattern to its natural conclusion, you'll find yourself thinking, *If only she'd grow up and move away, I'd be much happier.* No mom wants that kind of track record.

Tomorrow will bring a fresh challenge to take the place of the one you're dealing with today. Appreciate the now as much as you're able, which will provide your best insurance against later regrets.

The question is, how can I possibly do all I have to do if I move through my days at a snail's pace?

The answer is to lower your expectations.

These are not the years for the white-glove test, running a gloved hand atop picture frames to see if they're dust free. Let go of the fantasy that your home will be suitable for a decorating magazine while you raise young children. Kids are messy and not just at mealtimes. As they exercise creativity or experiment with new skills, messes are the norm. Even their best attempts at cleaning usually leave messes behind.

Lowering your expectations doesn't mean you have to live in a pigsty, and there will be times when you work together to get back to zero, putting everything away and actually cleaning. But if you bring out the vacuum every time your children leave their mark, you'll put yourself in bondage.

Lowering expectations is a good idea at mealtimes too. Though you may want to try new recipes now and then, remember that it's just fine to repeat your family's ten favorite meals over and over. They'll compliment your cooking and clean their plates.

In what other areas of mothering can you relax your standards? How about the laundry? Ideally, we like to see each child wearing freshly washed clothes daily, including our infants (who sometimes need multiple outfits). That philosophy creates mountains of laundry to gather, wash, dry, fold, and put away. Adopt the mindset that not every piece of clothing that's been worn needs to go into the hamper. Maybe those jeans can be used again tomorrow and the next day. Pajamas hold up well several nights in a row, and your children will thank you for allowing them to don their favorites more often.

And then there's your phone. Checking and rechecking social media can rob you of precious parenting minutes and produce frustration when your children need you and your attention is divided. Can you limit checking to certain times of the day or set limits on your minutes of screen time? Keep a week's log of how often you glance at your phone each day. You may be surprised.

You've been called to motherhood, and lowering standards that are too high for these "best years" is a big step toward being successful in this lofty calling. So after you've slowed your pace and lowered your expectations, what else can you do?

Practical Ways to Reduce Stress

- Pencil in some mommy time.
- Resist feeling guilty for alone time.
- Nap with your little ones.
- Ask your husband to help.
- Listen to worship music.
- Go to bed earlier.
- Enjoy a piece of chocolate.

I (Mary) was pregnant with Karl, who would be joining two siblings, three-year-old Luke and one-year-old Julia. Wanting to keep my skills fresh as a hospital nurse, I bought into the lie that a young mom can do it all. I figured the way to accomplish this was to work the night shift. After all, babies and toddlers still nap during the day, and I could catch up on sleep then.

But one person can't do the work of two.

I'll never forget one morning after working all night when I was nearly cross-eyed with fatigue. After my husband left for work, I came up with a plan to get some desperately needed sleep. I locked my two children and myself in our bedroom, figuring I could rest while they played. After all, there was nothing dangerous in the room. How wrong I was.

Although I hadn't planned to sleep, in just a minute I was out cold. It didn't last long, though, as a loud crash, followed by the wails of Julia, woke me with a start. I found my baby lying on the floor, bleeding from a gash on her cheek. Somehow she'd managed to pull over a portable wooden crib, which grazed her face on its way to the floor.

After the crisis passed, I suffered terrible guilt. Every time I looked at Julia's face, I was reminded of how foolish I'd been to think I could do it all. I failed at motherhood that day and learned a valuable lesson: no one can work all day and all night too. The day after Julia was injured, I quit my nursing job.

Every young mother works hard every day, all day. And if your desire is to find success in mothering, you'll have to repeatedly check your priorities. What's at the top of the list for you? What follows that? How is your time being spent? And your limited energy?

Once you answer those questions, ask yourself if there are any commitments you can trim during these busy years of mothering. Maybe other people can help you. Would your husband be willing to take over some of the tasks you regularly do? Could your church or neighborhood responsibilities be delegated to a friend or coworker? Might some of your commitments be put off until a later date? Figure out what you can let go of, and then let them go without guilt.

After you've lightened your load, ask yourself whether your priorities need a fresh look. It's possible your top priority ought to be sleep, since a tired mama is a cranky mama who doesn't cope well. Or you may need to improve your eating habits in order to feel better physically. What about arranging extra time with your husband by establishing a regular date night? This can work nicely even if you stay home and structure your date "after hours." Or, depending on your finances, you might consider hiring a sitter to have some uninterrupted time together.

And in terms of priorities, what about your devotional life? Be careful not to let time alone with God quietly sink to the bottom of your list.

Sample Priority List

- Time alone with God
- Adequate sleep
- Healthy food
- Date night
- Adult conversation
- Scriptural promises
- A trimmed schedule

Once you decide what's most important to you, set aside whatever is in the way of keeping those commitments. It'll take time to get where you want to be. But if you let your priorities dictate everything else, it *will* happen. And a sweet byproduct will be your fresh enjoyment of the children God gave you.

One other thing both of us found helpful was spending time with a mother-mentor. Keep your eyes peeled for possibilities, perhaps someone you already know. A mentor should be a woman you admire for her Christian character and love of family. How does she relate to her children and to those of others? Ideally, she will be about a decade ahead of you in her mothering, although it can work with someone older, too.

After you've chosen your would-be mentor (but haven't yet approached her), dialogue with God about her. Ask several important questions: "Will this person be an encouraging voice for me? Will her advice be grounded in godly wisdom? Might she fulfill a counseling role in regard to my mothering problems? Does she have a sense of humor? Does she walk closely with the Lord?"

Once you've prayed about it, expect God to give you the answers to your questions, along with the "when" and "how" of approaching her. Many mature women are willing to meet with younger moms, but if they aren't asked, they won't initiate it. That part is up to you.

A Good Mentor Is

- Experienced
- Wise
- Willing
- Hand-picked
- Seasoned
- Godly

It might seem scary to ask someone to mentor you, so just think of it as an invitation to a one-on-one conversation. Our suggestion would be to avoid directly asking for mentorship. Instead, ask if she'd be willing to drop by for a cup of coffee some time. Offer a few possible dates and see how she responds.

You might say you want to "pick her brain" about mothering, knowing she's a bit farther along than you. Then, if she agrees to come, have your questions ready. "When you had a child the age of mine, how did you handle such-and-such?" or "I'm expecting our second baby and am worried I won't love him as much as I did the first. Did you ever feel like that?"

Ask her to recount her own mothering experience. She'll be delighted that you want to know. If your time together goes well, ask if she'd like to meet again some time, and set a date. Eventually you'll get on a regular schedule and your time together will take on some structure. She'll begin praying for you and will become a friend to your children. But lest you worry that you'll always be the one receiving while she does all the giving, know that mentors are usually blessed by sharing their lives with their mentees.

The Bible urges older women to teach younger ones, so your mentor's obedience to this instruction will bring her a reward. She may feel unworthy to give advice or reluctant to call herself a mentor, but very few will turn down an invitation to chat over a cup of coffee. Consider also that this woman may feel honored that you want to hear from her.

CO-PARENTING WITH GOD

Lastly, in your effort to succeed at mothering, be sure to take advantage of your very best asset: the Lord. Remind yourself often that your children don't really belong to you but to Him. After all, by the time you found out you were pregnant, He had already been secretly at work for many days. According to the Bible, throughout those nine months God was quite active in your womb, establishing your child's personality, will, temperament, and much more, by way of DNA. He was actively weaving your baby's parts together, readying him for life on earth. Though God did include you in the process, the end result was really a compilation of His choices.

Once your baby is born, it doesn't make sense that the Lord would step aside and let you own His project. He gave you a critical role to play as the mother, and His hope is high that you'll invite Him to share in your efforts. He knows it's a big job with far-reaching consequences, so He offers to help.

It makes perfect sense that God wants to share in the responsibility of raising His children. And on those days when the heavy emotional weight of motherhood settles over you, He wants to share in that too.

As you manage your children day to day, the Lord gives you a wide berth to be as creative as you like. But it makes sense to bring Him into the entirety of your mothering, since He knows your children even better than you do. He created each one to be exactly as they are, placing them into your care, not someone else's. He equipped you with everything you need to raise them, and He believes you will do an excellent job. God sees every child as a major blessing, and He actually died to save them. Everything that happens to and around them is keenly important to Him.

So when you're struggling with something, whatever it is, ask Him what you should do. He is *the* Creator, and His supply of ideas never runs dry. If you ask, He'll put one of them into your head. And because He has never failed, if you follow His instructions, that idea is bound to work.

Every morning, even before your feet hit the floor, draw the Lord into your day and into your work as a mother. Start by breathing a quick prayer of thanks that He watched over you and your family during the night. Then ask Him to partner with you through the upcoming hours of your day. Scripture says "He gently leads those that have young" (Isaiah 40:11). This is you. As you submit to God's leadership, He'll either remove the obstacles you come up against or show you how to deal with them.

God honors submission and will bless you for letting Him take the lead. Acknowledge His sovereignty over your circumstances and defer to His plans for you and your family. And through your obedience, He will bless you.

LEARNING FROM FAILURE

No one does a perfect job of mothering, and there are days when failures outnumber successes. When that happens, how do you sidestep regrets that can sap your enthusiasm and instead direct your energy toward learning from failure?

I (Mary) remember one Sunday that was so complicated we had to go to church in shifts. We lived forty-five minutes away, so every Sunday morning seemed long. By 1:00 p.m. our children were always tired and anxious to get home for lunch. On this particular Sunday, we decided to eat at a restaurant, hoping our little ones would make it through without dozing in their chairs. Staying awake was critical to naptime later.

After lunch we drove both carloads home, and I got ready to put two-year-old Andrew to bed. When he was nowhere to be found, we realized we hadn't seen him since the restaurant, and a cold shiver ran up my spine.

Quickly, we called the restaurant, and sure enough, our little guy was unharmed and happy in the care of the cashier. But it could have been a disaster. Andrew might have run out the door and into the street, where four lanes of traffic would have had devastating results. He might have panicked, yelling, "Mommy! Mommy!" which would have let everyone know he was alone.

When we walked in, expecting tears, Andrew greeted us with, "I got gum."

Thankfully he was fine, though the incident did take a toll on me. I'm ashamed to say I repeated this same troublesome mothering failure several more times before finally learning to keep better watch over my little ones.

Remember that failure can teach important lessons. At times we can't figure out how to do something right until we've done it wrong first. This is especially true if we have a false sense of confidence about our parenting skills and plow ahead without thinking things through. In that case, failure can effectively convince us we didn't know as much as we thought.

Please know that though your mothering intention might be pure, failure can occur anyway. When it does, be quick to accept the blame, but don't let regret fill you with sadness. Instead, seek to learn from your mistakes and ask the Lord to show you how to do better.

A Path to Success

- Partner with God.
- Slow your pace.
- Lower your expectations.
- Cut unnecessary commitments.
- Prioritize.
- Enlist help.
- Find a mentor.
- Enjoy your children.

God says if you humble yourself under His hand, He will lift you up when the time is right (1 Peter 5:5–7). Meanwhile, He promises to give you the grace to get through even repeated failures of the same dilemma. As you submit to His leadership, you'll find yourself meeting with success more and more, and these "best years" are bound to become better and better.

The Lord upholds all who fall
and lifts up all who are bowed down.
Psalm 145:14

What can you do today?
Study your child while he's asleep and marvel over his beauty.

We wish we'd known . . .
1. we would stumble.
2. the "best years" were over quicker than we thought.
3. to appreciate the blessings of the "best years."

Chapter 3

TAKE TIME TO TEACH

Be very careful, then, how you live—
not as unwise but as wise, making the most of every opportunity.
Ephesians 5:15–16

I (Mary) knew that as a mom it was my responsibility to "train up my child in the way he should go" as the old King James Version puts it (Proverbs 22:6). So I got busy with my kids, preschoolers included, teaching them to make their beds. I knew once they mastered that, they'd feel good about themselves, and I'd feel good about giving them a valuable habit they could use the rest of their lives.

Knowing young children can't be expected to do well at chores beyond their capabilities, I simplified the process to include only a fitted sheet, a blanket, and a pillow, never expecting them to *change* the sheets, just to make the beds.

I gathered the children and said, "I'm going to show you how to make your own beds."

They responded with enthusiasm. "I wanna try!"

But day after day, the beds remained unmade, so I thought I'd sweeten the deal. "Who wants a candy treat?"

Again, enthusiasm prevailed.

"When I see your beds made, I'll put a candy on your pillow."

They all agreed.

I thought bed-making could be learned after just one lesson, but even with the candy, most of the kids worked at it for weeks before faithfully doing it, sometimes taxing my patience. In the end, only Andrew adopted it as a regular habit. His room was often in shambles, but his bed was always made.

Now Is the Time to Teach

Teaching children is a laborious task that requires infinite time and patience. Whether it's demonstrating a new skill, describing a new responsibility, or explaining a new family rule, one lesson usually won't do it—that is, unless *they're* the ones initiating the tutoring session. When that happens, your percentage of success skyrockets.

I (Margaret) remember watching two-year-old Lars struggle with a simple toy train, trying to hook four cars together. It was a toy made for a child of his age, but he didn't understand that each car had to be turned the same direction, with its hook facing the engine. Although two hooks could be attached, the next attachment of two rings wouldn't work.

He became frustrated and really wanted to do it, so I set aside my own project and got down on the floor with him. After demonstrating how to succeed and how to fail, and after putting my hand over his to turn each car as needed, he got it. Because he wanted to learn it, he quickly did, in less than ten minutes.

When little ones watch what their mothers are doing and say, "Mommy, can I do that too?" most moms groan. Stopping what you're doing to teach a skill that a child may or may not be ready for often taxes a mother's patience and ends in a bigger mess than she was tackling at the beginning. But children are more capable than we think, earlier than we think, and with careful instruction they can often impress us. And if they're the ones initiating the lesson, success is more likely.

Moms usually race through their days trying to accomplish forty-eight hours' worth of work in twenty-four, and it's often the children who get shortchanged. Being in a hurry is the enemy of teaching children; slowing down is a parenting ally. If we're not careful, we can see our youngsters as obstacles to how we really want to spend our time. But if we find ourselves thinking this way, we ought to remember the value of those little ones in God's sight. Very few things on a calendar compare with the importance of spending time teaching children. Reassessing priorities every so often is valuable.

I (Mary) recall teaching my sixth child to tie her shoes when she was three and a half. Stina wanted to learn this new skill, so I determined to say yes to coaching her each time she wanted to try again. Tying bows is complicated, and we worked on it over and over. We used table legs, chair legs, my shoes, and finally her shoes. It took longer than I thought, but because she had the want-to, she also had the perseverance to see it through.

But what if I had pulled away from her, frustrated with her inability to learn? I might have said, "Stina, you're too young to figure this out. Wait till you're older. You can't do it now."

That was tempting, since it did seem she was unable to master it, and I grew tired of working with her. But quitting too soon would have taught her something I didn't want her to learn—that when a job gets difficult, it's OK to quit. Although our teaching sessions were all about shoelaces, beneath the surface Stina was catching other things. Persevering through struggle was one, and a second was that I loved her enough to keep helping her.

Had I given up, the subtle message would have been, "Stina, I've given you enough time on this, and I don't want to spend any more on it." And since children spell love T-I-M-E, what she would have heard would have been, "Mom loves me, but her love is limited." I would never have wanted her to feel that way. If you can manage it, the best time to teach is now.

Teaching Takes Time

All mothers of young children know what it means to live an interrupted life. Focusing on your own work is almost impossible if your child is interrupting with endless demands. But the most common explanation behind constant disruptions is a heightened need for mom's focused attention. A mother's highest priority ought to be training her children, particularly when they're little. During their first five years, they're putty in your hands, compared to later when they'll reason that their own ideas (and those of their peers) are better than yours.

A PEEK INTO YOUR PRESCHOOLER'S HEART

- My universe revolves around me.
- My world is often confusing.
- I can't trust everyone.
- Sometimes I'm afraid.
- A night-light is comforting.
- My world is new and interesting.
- I like to go along.
- I learn fast.
- I can't verbalize how I feel.
- I adore my mother.
- I want to do what Mommy does.

That's one reason it's important to spend chunks of time with them when they're little, which includes those pesky interruptions. Rather than figuring out a way to get rid of them when they repeatedly disrupt you, try taking a minute to engage. Grab her for a quick hug and kiss, which can bring an end to the interruption. Tell him, "I love you sooo much" face-to-face, another valuable way to connect in just a few seconds. If they hear, "Mommy is busy. Stop bothering me," it's the same as hearing, "Lots of other things are more important than you."

Teaching children takes gobs of time, and often you'll wonder where in the world you're going to find it. But their all-time favorite thing to do is spend time with you. And if you're willing to do that, you'll be communicating love in a way all children understand.

POTENTIAL FOR EVERY DAY

- Hug your child.
- Say I love you.
- Praise your child.
- Compliment your child for any job done.
- Kiss your child.
- Tell him you're glad he's yours.

One way to spend time together and still get something done is to let them help you. Though that thought might make you cringe, if you take time to simplify certain household chores, even your toddlers can learn how.

At our house (Margaret's), when each child turned two, they stopped *being* a chore, and their name went on the chore chart as a doer. This meant they had little jobs to do every week, and at the end of the week they were rewarded for successes (a candy treat, an inexpensive trinket, allowance—never more than one-fourth their age). I tried to keep their assignments level with their skills, which, of course, were minimal. Often their jobs had to be redone later, but I never let them see that happen.

One chore they all loved was getting the day's mail from our country mailbox, which was separated from the house by about fifty feet. The job required that they carry a small plastic stool (since the mailbox was too high for them to reach all the way in) and a small shopping bag to carry the mail back to the house.

Learning the process took several instructional sessions, and even after each one learned it, there were often crises. A letter might blow away. Falling down might bring tears and abandonment of the stool and/or bag of mail. Slippery snow might cause trouble. And of course each of these morphed into another interruption for me. But it wasn't just about getting the mail into the house. It was teaching these young children about pulling together as a family to get the work done. It was also an antidote to laziness. Everybody was part of the family team, which made the younger set feel important. To this day my kids remember chore charts with fondness.

TEACHING WITHOUT WORDS

Teaching children how to work is only the beginning. Your youngsters are watching you every minute, absorbing lessons tied to your behavior. Whether it's intentional or not, they're always learning from you, and some of the things they're learning by observation are far more significant than making beds or collecting mail. Watching you move through your day as you respond to mini emergencies, do your own work, or have conversations with others teaches all kinds of things. They learn when it's OK to be frenzied or calm, angry or pleasant, kind or unkind, rough or gentle, honest or dishonest.

Since children learn what is caught, not taught, modeling positive character traits should always be on a mother's mind. As you live out everyday life in front of your children, make the decision to exemplify the attributes you hope your youngsters will one day have.

I (Mary) remember being watched by four-year-old Jo as I cared for her new baby sister, Stina, the one who came after her. She learned that when babies are crying, their mommies usually pick them up. It was something she internalized simply by observing.

As children grow from babies into preschoolers, they'll watch so closely they will sometimes point out inconsistencies. "Mommy, the baby is crying. You should pick her up." Evidence of what children are learning from a mother's example can also be seen by how they play with their toys. What do they say to their baby dolls? How do they handle their toy cars? What kinds of interactions take place between your children and others?

Young children mimic what they see, which then allows us a glimpse into what kind of mothers we are. What is the legacy you'll leave for your kids? What will they remember as most important to you?

Their nonstop scrutiny can seem like a burden, but it's also an ongoing opportunity to improve your teaching. Part of God's plan in sending little observers to mothers is to challenge those moms to make improvements in their own lives. It forces them to ask, "Is my behavior (or are my habits) teaching my kids to live upright lives? Or am I compromising good values by what I do and say, lowering the bar for them?"

Make a list of character traits you'd like to see in your children. Then, if your own conduct doesn't line up with what's on the list, make corrections where needed. As you implement changes, you'll benefit your children and better yourself. Scripture encourages us to live lives that are blameless and pure so we'll be shining examples of God's children (Philippians 2:15). First and foremost, we're to do this in front of our children.

CHARACTER TRAITS TO MODEL

- Integrity
- Cheerfulness
- Kindness
- Patience
- Gratitude
- Diligence
- Perseverance
- Optimism
- Forgiveness

BE A PATIENT TEACHER

I (Margaret) remember a family vacation to Florida during which a golden opportunity to teach presented itself through our toddler, Hans, two and a half at the time. We were walking to the beach when he spotted a chubby caterpillar inching its way across the sidewalk. Bending over to take a closer look, Hans planted his hands on either side of this wiggling phenomenon, his diapered rear end in the air.

It was one of thousands of teachable moments that presented itself in the life of just this one child. I knelt down next to him to see what he was seeing and made a few simple comments, linking God to the little caterpillar and letting Hans take all the time he wanted to watch it move. I didn't know exactly what he was thinking, since two-year-olds don't have extensive language, but he said enough to let me know he was positively impressed.

I wish I could say I was always that patient when teachable moments popped up. No doubt being on vacation had something to do with a slower pace on caterpillar day, but it remains an example to me of how a less hurried life can be a gift to children.

Often when a young child is whining, it's because we're either pushing them through their day or pushing them out of our way. Pursuing a schedule that is jam-packed assures we won't have even a couple of minutes to let our little people take life at their preferred, snail-slow pace. Rushing a child frustrates them to the same degree it frustrates us when hurried through a project. *If only I had more time*, we think. The same is true for children.

Examine your commitments with ruthless honesty. Don't let them overwhelm your intent to be a good mother. Your children are with you for only a short time, and though it's difficult to believe now, a day will come when they're grown and you'll have all kinds of extra time. Make the decision to decelerate in favor of more time at kid-level, eye to eye, letting them set the pace whenever possible. Someday, looking back from the vantage point of an empty nest, you'll be thankful you did.

Teach Your Family's History

Psalm 145:13 says, "Your kingdom is an everlasting kingdom, and your dominion endures through all generations."

As a mother, you're steadily working on teaching your children this marvelous phenomenon, that God's sovereignty blankets your family, the families who've come before yours, and the ones yet to come. Though this sounds like a formidable task, broken into small bites it can be great fun.

One way we've worked at this is to annually visit the cemetery where several family members are buried. Our children loved this tradition as toddlers, and now that they're grown, they still work hard to be there each year. We schedule our cemetery trip every Memorial Day weekend, coupling it with a picnic in a nearby park or a trip to McDonald's.

Our parents taught us that death is part of life, and loving Jesus negates all fear. As we stand around the tombstones each year, older members in our extended family tell stories about those buried there, people who lived and died long before we came along. Each life has a story, and by listening to the details we've gotten to know them. Our preschool children have especially enjoyed looking at pictures of these people, which we bring along when we visit.

We've continued the tradition with our fourteen children (plus our brother's three), and the stories handed down through the generations have become living testimonies to the relatives buried there. Though we'll never know them in this life, we'll meet them all in heaven.

Your children crave security, and you can give it to them by describing the joy that comes after physical death when we know and love Jesus.

You can talk about your own grandparents, great-aunts or great-uncles, any who have died, making sure to count blessings in relation to their lives. If your ancestors didn't live stellar lives, you have an opportunity to discuss that too. Talk openly with your children and answer their questions honestly—four- and five-year-olds are especially warm to spiritual things—and use a lighthearted voice.

Remind them that Jesus is the one who can hold a family together because He's the only constant through all generations. Though you might have to say goodbye to Grandma or Grandpa, Jesus will be with you always. Tell them He never changes and is the same yesterday and today and forever (Hebrews 13:8). A cemetery is a natural place to present the gospel to your children, along with God's rich promises for life after death. Pray together, thanking the Lord for giving life, for loving us, and for making it possible for anyone who believes in Jesus to go to heaven after they die (John 11:25).

By the way, be sure to leave the cemetery before closing time, when they lock the gates. (We learned that the hard way.)

Another way to recognize your roots is to celebrate the country or countries your ancestors came from. America is unique in that our families originated someplace else. You might want to establish an annual dinner, serving the foods of your ethnic roots. Label them in the language of that nation and teach those food words to your little ones. Decorate as these ancestors would have, letting your children make banners, streamers, bunting, or whatever else that culture enjoyed.

On a map or globe, show them where that country is and talk up the differences. Put outfits together that reflect what children wore in that place at that time, and learn one of their childhood dances or songs. How did they celebrate birthdays, Christmas, or the arrival of a new baby? With the advantage of the internet, ethnic research is at your fingertips.

Another meaningful project is to make a family tree. You could use a leafless branch from outdoors, hanging paper names high and low to represent different generations. Use first names only for your preschoolers, but you'll be surprised at how they'll remember who's who.

And never miss a chance to point to the places where Jesus made a difference. We've found letters written in the late 1800s by relatives who made reference to Christ and the decisions they made according to His will. These become treasured markers in your family's history, encouraging you as a mom—and your children as the next generation—to continue following the Lord. Who knows but one of those ancestors prayed "for those yet unborn" to come to Christ. And here you are . . .

Visiting the cemetery is but one of hundreds of traditions you might want to establish in your family. We do have one caution, though. Consider the end before you begin. Watch out for those that might become expensive or in some other way grow into a burden. Think small. Start with little stabs at exploring how your ancestors did things, and give them a chance to morph into tried-and-true traditions as you tweak them over time. If something just doesn't click, let it go.

If you have warm memories of special times in your own family, start there. Then you can make the choice to jump on the bandwagon of the biggest, most popular holidays, or you can zero in on some that get short shrift: President's Day, May Day, the first day of a new season, Labor Day, Columbus Day, and others. Children love the anticipation, the celebration itself, and the reminiscing afterward. They also love repetition, especially of a good time. Repeat that good time twice in a row, and you've got a new family tradition.

TRADITIONS . . . CONSIDER THIS:

- Will the idea work as my child gets older?
- Will it become costly if continued through childhood?
- Will it be workable with more than one child?
- Will it take more of my time as I have less of it?
- Will it require increased storage space?

As you establish family traditions, reshuffle or change them in any way you like while your children are still young. They'll never miss what you subtract. Make your occasions work for you rather than against you. Never continue doing something that isn't working just because you started that way. Remember the guy who kept banging his head against the wall because it felt so good when he stopped?

And one final word. If you aren't sure where to start, look at families you know who enjoy spending time together. What do they do? When? How? Why? Ask questions. They'll be honored you noticed and won't mind a bit if you copy. Little by little, whatever you decide to do will evolve into special times unique to your family. The important thing is to get started.

GOD IS A MOTHER'S TEACHER

I (Mary) was blessed with three children in less than four years, and I took for granted that we could have more babies anytime we wanted. But the next pregnancy ended in miscarriage. And the one after that too. I wondered if three children were all we were meant to have.

Six years later, though, Andrew came along. This pregnancy threatened to miscarry also, but he finally arrived, safe and sound, and my joy knew no bounds. As I gazed at his freshly scrubbed newborn face, I was overcome with wonder at how this could be. I'd had two miscarriages followed by an endangered pregnancy, yet here he was, in my arms.

The everyday noises of the hospital environment faded into the background as I took in the wonder of this brand-new child, a gift of incalculable worth. And at that moment Teacher-God taught me an important lesson I've not forgotten. Using my baby as His visual aid, He said, "Yes, you're holding a miracle, but don't get lost in the wonder of this particular baby. *Every* baby is a miracle. My miracle. Though your first three came easily, don't ever forget that *each* child is a wonder."

I've thought of that moment hundreds of times, learning to apply the lesson to each of my seven children. But that's not all. God wanted me to see that He meant it for everyone else's children too. No child is unwanted by Him, and every life is His miracle. Each one is equally valuable to Him, and He wanted me to view all children in that way.

When God sends babies into our homes, He has much to teach us through their presence and quickly enrolls us in His school of learning. Though He wants us to learn about Himself as God the Father while we parent our children, He also wants to teach us how to teach them. The Bible includes innumerable references to parents, appealing to our everyday experiences. This makes it easier for us to put flesh on His valuable lessons.

For example, Isaiah 49:15 teaches that God will never forget us or leave us hanging, modeling how we're to act toward our children. Directing His words specifically to mothers, He paints a word picture we can appreciate: "Can a mother forget the baby at her breast and have no compassion on the child she has borne? Though she may forget, I will not forget you!"

His words parallel an important mothering principle. No nursing mother can forget she has a baby, because the replenishing of mother's milk is her constant reminder. In the same way but even more so, God will never forget us. And in this teaching, He's letting us know we ought to express the same truth to those in our care. We're to make truth "stick" by bringing it down to the level of those we're teaching. If we use everyday words and examples, children will learn it faster and it'll stick longer.

We also learn from Scripture what patient parental teaching looks like. In Genesis 2, the Lord lets Adam, the first human being, name all the animals God had formed from the ground. These animals belonged to God. He shaped them and established their characteristics, and certainly He could have named them Himself, probably with more creativity than Adam used. But He let Adam "help" with this important task.

Verse 19 says, "He brought them to the man to see what he would name them; and whatever the man called each living creature, that was its name." God didn't make suggestions during the process or redo any of the names when Adam was finished. He didn't interfere in any way. Instead He gave Adam complete freedom to do the job in whatever way he chose. And afterward, He let it stand.

This challenges today's mothers to let their children participate in important jobs. They should give them the freedom to do it the way they believe is best, even if that way might turn out poorly. In the end, the greater value might not have been in the task accomplished but in the lessons learned along the way.

When God let Adam name the animals, He was teaching on multiple levels. It's possible one of the reasons He wanted this first man to study each animal was to have a lightbulb moment somewhere in the process, when it would occur to Adam that none of them were like him. "Wow! These animals are all different from each other, but *I'm* something else again! I'm actually more akin to God's image than to theirs."

And when God finally presented Eve to Adam, the impact of meeting her after studying all the animals would surely have been more powerful as he recognized she was "something else" too!

Have you ever wondered how long it took for Adam to give unique names to "all the livestock, the birds in the sky, and all the wild animals" (Genesis 2:20)? God's patience is a wonderful model for mothers as they teach their children. The Creator had several important things for Adam to learn when He invited him to name the animals, just as you have multiple things for your children to learn in any given life experience. Patient waiting is always one of the hallmarks of a good teacher.

TEACHING TACTICS OF THE MASTER

- Love your pupils.
- Accept them as they are.
- Look them in the eye.
- Keep lessons short.
- Be gentle.
- Tell stories.
- Use visual aids.
- Pray for your students.

God shows moms how to teach their children in one more way—through getting to know Jesus. In the Bible, children loved Jesus, and don't you wonder why? Maybe they knew He accepted them just as they were, so they felt the depth of His love for them.

Maybe He drew them in with His eye-to-eye focus. Maybe they were won over by His gentle touch. Maybe it was the interesting stories He told or the way He used visual aids. Or maybe it was that He didn't lecture but drew them in with questions. Whatever the reason, it seems children loved listening to Jesus. And moms will find their children love listening to them, too, if they teach in those same ways.

We can learn the how-tos of effective teaching by watching both God and Jesus, but it means taking time to study the Bible. Adopting the tried-and-true methods of a Master Teacher will not only guarantee good results, it'll relieve you of having to come up with your own lesson plans. And if you ever bump into a teaching dilemma you don't know how to handle, just ask the expert. "Show me your ways, Lord, teach me your paths. Guide me in your truth and teach me, for you are God my Savior, and my hope is in you all day long" (Psalm 25:4–5).

God the Father and Jesus the Son want to share their teaching ideas with you, and becoming a good teacher starts with being a good student.

> *Be strong and courageous,*
> *because you will lead these people.*
> Joshua 1:6

What can you do today?
Identify one thing you're eager to teach your child tomorrow.

What we wish we'd known . . .
1. our children were learning from us every minute.
2. our children were capable of learning earlier than we thought.
3. less is more with young children.

Chapter 4

KEEP ALL YOUR PLATES SPINNING

I have learned the secret of being content in any and every situation.
I can do all this through him who gives me strength.
Philippians 4:12–13

Have you ever seen one of those circus acts where a man spins a breakable plate atop a wiggly pole and then tries to keep it (and many others) twirling simultaneously? He darts back and forth behind a long table, jiggling the sticks just enough to rev up each plate for a few more seconds. If he doesn't get back to one of them in time, the plate falls and breaks.

Mothers of young children often feel just like that plate-spinning performer, racing from one high-pressure responsibility to another, making quick decisions, hoping they don't miss anything important. If they can't move fast enough or miss a commitment, they fear something will shatter.

When I (Margaret) learned I was pregnant for the first time, a warm glow flooded through me. I felt as if I'd spent my whole life preparing for motherhood, preferring dolls to other toys, and I prayed every night that my favorite baby doll would come to life. In grade school I fantasized about having eight children someday, and I chose names for each one. In photos from my childhood, I'm usually the one holding a baby, and as soon as I was able, I began babysitting for other people's children. I knew I had a knack with kids and couldn't have been more eager to become a mother.

And then my baby was born. No one told me how edgy I'd feel at the screechy cry of a newborn or how I'd suffer when I couldn't make him happy. And it had never occurred to me I'd have more questions than answers. Worst of all, though, was the day I first felt the full weight of motherhood's responsibilities settling on me, and I just couldn't stop crying.

My plates began to wobble.

As I dashed about trying to feed, bathe, and dress my very fussy newborn, I found I couldn't feed, bathe, and dress myself. And there were lots of other "plates" too: visitors, thank-you notes, housecleaning, errand running, meal prep, and keeping my husband happy. How could I do all that when I couldn't even get my teeth brushed till he came home from work?

All new moms find themselves in this kind of spin, wondering how they'll ever keep it up. We can put an extra toothbrush in a kitchen drawer, but what about the bigger issues?

What about exhaustion and the negativity that comes with it? How about the battle against kiddie clutter? Or the frustration of not having enough time to finish what's been started or do any one job well? Many moms also find themselves spinning in a new kind of loneliness, feeling isolated from the real world. And sometimes they feel spiritual loneliness, too, unable to connect with God while keeping their plates spinning.

FIGHTING FATIGUE

Most busy mommies can tell tales of exhaustion so deep that they've fallen asleep at stoplights or in the middle of phone conversations. I (Margaret) remember sleep taking over while reading a story to my two preschoolers. I could hear myself slurring words, but despite my best efforts, exhaustion was having its way. My last semiconscious thought was to hope I could actually continue reading while I slept. But the children, with their poking and nudging, didn't let me find out. "Mommy! Keep going!" And that's what weary mommies do. They just keep going.

I (Mary) remember the love affair I had with my pillow during those tiring days. After an up-and-down night of dealing with a wakeful newborn and a sleep-resistant toddler, I felt worn out even before my feet hit the floor. I longed for more sleep, but little children have no concept of a mother's needs. So after dragging myself out of bed each morning, I'd turn around and pat my pillow, sometimes even talking to it. "I can't wait to get back to you," I'd say, knowing that wouldn't be for many hours.

During this fatiguing time, God gave me a good idea. Each day at rest time, I could climb on the bed between two little nappers, which had two benefits. It helped me police the children, making sure no shenanigans kept them from resting, and as they quieted down, I did too, dozing off quickly. When I would wake ten minutes later, the children were both asleep and my power nap had refreshed me enough to make it through the hours ahead.

Moms can grab forty winks in other places too, like if they arrive home with children asleep in their car seats. Why not join them for a few minutes? Both of us have slept in dentist chairs, while giving blood, and, yes, in church. The back row often has a special benefit: a wall to rest your head on.

I (Margaret) discovered that one more way to gain energy during those worn-and-weary days was to eat right. Though first choice was to consume a long row of Oreo cookies for lunch, my body did better with leftovers from dinner the night before or a ham and cheese sandwich. Vitamins helped too. And lots of strong, black coffee.

When we were awash with fatigue from being up with babies during the night, we sisters would always check in by phone the next morning. "How was your night?"

Although some of these exchanges had colorful answers, more often than not one of us would say, "I can't really remember if I was up or not!"

Maybe it was the fatigue talking, but my guess is that like many moms, we got so used to being tired we learned to function within it and hardly noticed. Surely that's God's gift to young mothers.

During these sleep-deprived days, it's important to remember two things: one, the exhaustion of young motherhood will end one day, and two, if you ever find yourself able to get a good nap, do it without guilt. It'll bring you back to square one.

But weary or rested, remember that your hard work as a mother is never wasted.

ENCOURAGEMENT FOR MOM

- You are equipped to mother your child.
- Your child is a gift from God.
- You know your child best.
- Your work as a mom is never wasted.
- You are God to your child.
- You are never alone.
- You are loved by the Creator.
- Your refreshment will come from God's Word.

FIGHTING DISORDER

When a first child arrives, living life in an orderly way goes out the window. Though we do our best to organize our babies and toddlers, it isn't long before we find out motherhood comes at the expense of a neat, tidy existence.

How well I (Margaret) remember the day two-year-old Louisa jammed the drinking-water button *inside* our refrigerator. When I opened it ten minutes later, the water had filled to the third shelf, which hit me like an icy tidal wave. Cleanup meant an overhaul of the entire kitchen and refrigerator, two time-consuming chores on an already jam-packed day.

Before children, women can prioritize orderly to-do lists and tackle the items one by one, often from start to finish. But after little ones arrive, every day is chopped into small bits of several minutes apiece, which can cause tremendous frustration. And interruptions? They're constant.

You might say, "But my Motherhood Mission Statement is taped to my desk, and I'm going to follow that." Before you became a mom, those words were a banner of assured triumph, but babies can't read. Even if they could, it wouldn't matter, since they come with a firmly intact banner of their own. It says ME AHEAD OF YOU.

And that's not all. When you cradle your firstborn immediately after birth, little do you know then that the U-Haul truck parked outside the hospital loaded with baby gear belongs to him. After it follows you home, each item must be given its own parking spot within your once-organized living space.

At first you don't mind that your home resembles a Babies R Us outlet. You love the sight of your vibrating infant seat and battery-operated swing. But after you've tripped over them seventeen times, you're ready to kick them out the front door. So what can be done?

First of all, consider the end before you begin. Think practical. I (Mary) was expecting our first baby, Luke, when my husband and I went shopping with money we'd received at a baby shower. We fell in love with an expensive wooden high chair in sparkling white. If I could choose again, I'd buy one with a tray that wouldn't warp when soaked in a bathtub overnight to get the gunk off. I'd also consider a smaller one that didn't take up more room than an adult chair at our table and didn't have legs so wide it would trip me each time I walked past.

I (Margaret) felt well equipped for our firstborn's arrival. We had a baby bassinet for his early weeks, a portable crib for the months after that, and a full-size crib for the ensuing years. These three big items required that we find extra floor space by moving other things out of the way, things we didn't really want to move.

After baby Nelson came home, though, he spent his first weeks in our bed, skipping the bassinet, after which he skipped the portable crib and went straight to the bigger crib. So, two out of three were unnecessary.

Though beds are big-space items, even little things can get out of hand. Take toys, for example. Though it starts with a few tiny rattles, bigger babies require bigger toys. Eventually toys take over your life. You'll be stepping on them during the night and kicking them out of your way during the day. That's not to say we don't love to browse and buy in toy stores, making excess almost inevitable.

One helpful philosophy is to cap your inventory by subtracting one toy for each new one added. Whether the subtracted toy goes to Goodwill, the church nursery, or the trash, the principle is good and helps conquer clutter.

Controlling toy chaos can be done the same way we often control children. Put four preschoolers in a giant room and they'll quickly get wild, yelling, running, and knocking each other down. Put those same kids in a small room and they'll busy themselves with dolls, Matchbox cars, and puzzles: quieter activities.

Some moms segregate toys in large, covered bins, storing them in the garage, on a high shelf, or under a bed. Children can "check out" one or two bins at a time. Then, during play as the toys mix together and the kids want another, more orderly bin, cleanup must take place first. Since the mess is small, they can handle it, and clutter stays manageable.

What about the emotional and mental disorder that comes to every new mother? By necessity, her child becomes one of her highest priorities, which means that other things—things that still matter a great deal to her—must be pushed down the list.

Ask God to help you. He says that if we cast our burdens on Him, He'll sustain us (Psalm 55:22). He doesn't say He'll bring order, but that He'll keep us moving forward despite the mess. The word "sustain" means "to support, hold up, or keep someone going," exactly what young moms need. The Lord can show you how to function hour to hour without tearing out your hair. He can teach you to find humor in previously exasperating moments and will remind you often how important your mothering is—to your child and to Him.

As you're learning to let God sustain you, try to eliminate two words from your vocabulary: "efficiency" and "speed." Babies and young children pick up on your stress when you're trying to accomplish too much in a day, and they'll only make things more difficult for you as they demand your attention.

While you're calling to the Lord for help, a good word to add to your vocabulary is "slower." If you have too much to do, ask yourself if there's anything you can hand off to someone else. What can be eliminated? What is your husband willing to do? What can be postponed? What can be done in partnership with another mom?

Take a serious look at the reasons behind the disorder around you. After my toddler had flooded my fridge and I was transferring soggy food to the kitchen counter, I had to admit she hadn't jammed that button to destroy my schedule or make a mess. She was just doing what she'd seen others do. And that night as I put her to bed, I was thankful for a clean kitchen floor and a reorganized refrigerator.

FIGHTING NEGATIVITY

Little children give moms lots to complain about. They're messy, loud, demanding, and needy, and that's just on the good days. Coping with all of this is enough to send a young mom into a tizzy. I (Mary) am going to do a little true confessing here, sharing a motherhood moment I regret to this day, forty years after the fact.

Julia and Karl, ages three and two, were playing happily in the bathtub while I ran back and forth from the next room, working on a project and occasionally checking on them. When it was time to get out of the tub, I instructed them to put all the toys back into the basket, and then I went back into the next room. But when I returned a few minutes later, they had done just the opposite of my instructions. They'd thrown the toys (along with lots of water) all over the bathroom floor, laughing hard at their fun idea.

Because it was an overfull day and I was rushing, my response was far from ideal. I swung my leg back and kicked a plastic truck as hard as I could, flinging it above their heads into the tub wall where it broke into pieces. And it gets worse. Rather than remorse over my anger, my thought was, *That'll show 'em!* And I felt really good.

But several hours later I asked myself, *What good did that do? What did I teach them by losing my temper as I did?* Though neither of them remembers the incident, I certainly do, and I wish I'd shown more self-control. I missed an opportunity to model a quality character trait: forgiveness.

Maybe you, too, have found it difficult to fit the demands of children into your busy life. It was a shock to discover how many hours it took to care for a new baby, and the surprises never ended. The old adage that "a mother's work is never done" takes on new meaning, and you realize you're in a spin that's hard to slow down.

On a bad day when things stockpile and get too hectic to handle, you might be tempted to step back and let a few of your plates crash to the floor. After all, one person can only do so much. You find yourself complaining about overload, and even your husband doesn't fully understand. That's when it's a good idea to turn to the one who called you to motherhood in the first place, God Himself.

But how can an overloaded mom possibly find quiet time to pursue the Lord? Your little ones might start each day hours before you'd like them to, and their demands insist that your feet hit the floor running. How can you possibly sit down with your Bible or take time to pray?

Please know that God is watching you and thoroughly understands your dilemma. He witnesses every emergency, mistake, and crisis. He's aware of your time crunches. But He has nourishment and encouragement to hand to you if you'll reach for it.

God is willing to meet you in snippets of time rather than big chunks, and to act in power in response to short prayers breathed out in the middle of messy days. He knows what's possible and what isn't, and He will never ask you to do what you can't. But He wants you to acknowledge His presence and seek His advice. When you do, He promises to give it generously (James 1:5). And if all you can manage is to cry, "Help!" He'll respond quickly, faithfully, and in power.

Allowing ourselves big doses of negativity takes us to a place of sadness and frustration. I (Margaret) remember a day when I reached a new low. Klaus and Hans, two years old and nine months, respectively, both ate in high chairs. I was on my hands and knees wiping the floor beneath their chairs for the umpteenth time. It wasn't long before I was questioning the choices that had put me in that miserable place.

Self-pity had taken over, priming my pump with tears, and I did the only thing I thought would help me. I whined. Since the children didn't care that their mom was in a crisis, I took it straight to the top and whined to God. "Why do I have to do this so many times every day? No one appreciates it."

I was just getting started when the Lord stopped me.

It was as if He said, *OK then. Don't wipe the floor for your toddlers. Wipe it for me.* Scripture says, "Whatever you do, do it all for the glory of God" (1 Corinthians 10:31). In one concise statement He had crashed my pity party and elevated my grunt work to a divine level. Then, after I stopped feeling put upon, He gave me a few other potent thoughts.

He reminded me I had longed for those children and was very thankful for them. And I was glad I could stay home with them full time. The Lord had given me the desire of my heart, and I had responded by whining, which hadn't even helped. But once I began wiping the floor for God, I knew my work mattered. The bottom line was, He understood my frustration and gave me a way to cope.

Although a baby's needs can seem to engulf you, try to recognize that she's a treasure from God, and your sense of negativity will evaporate. No matter how rough it gets, if you're willing to view your children as His gifts, He'll take responsibility for bringing you through.

God considers children one of life's most valuable blessings. In the Bible, He often rewarded a woman by way of a newborn.

It's as if the best gift He could think of was arranging for women to raise, nurture, and love a child. Although the job can completely deplete us, He sees that as our opportunity to call for extra blessing, which He then joyfully delivers.

How *Not* to Achieve a Quiet Time

- Set unrealistic goals.
- Plan it to be at the end of the day.
- Count on an hour of uninterrupted time.
- Resent any interruption.
- Wait until you have an empty schedule.
- Give up when it doesn't go as planned.

The next time you're up during the night feeding a hungry newborn, resist the urge to make a mental list of complaints. Instead list what you find to be precious about him and thank the One who created him with those things, mentioning each one. Or study your baby's face in the dim glow of a night-light and thank God for each of her features. Softly hum a worship song or hymn as you rock your little one, reciting the words inside your head. Pray rich blessings over your baby, telling God what your hopes and dreams are for him. Name spiritual blessings you hope he will experience. Quote Scripture over him as you snuggle together.

VERSES TO PRAY OVER YOUR CHILDREN

- Psalm 119:72—to love God's Word
- Proverbs 10:9—to walk in integrity
- Proverbs 14:23—to work hard
- Psalm 107:1—to be thankful
- James 4:7—to resist the devil
- Proverbs 1:10—to choose friends wisely
- 1 John 1:9—to confess sin
- 2 Timothy 1:7—to have self-discipline
- Colossians 2:8—to believe only truth
- Psalm 3:5—to sleep well
- 1 John 5:13—to be eternally secure
- 1 Corinthians 10:13—to escape temptation

Turn those 3:00 a.m. feedings into something special, and you might even begin to value what you gain during these unique moments together. And please remember that as you hold your child, the Lord is holding you, looking at you through eyes of fervent love. As you cradle your child, He is cradling you . . . "in his everlasting arms" (Deuteronomy 33:27).

Both of us look back on the fatiguing months of young motherhood and say, "I wish I could go back to that special time with my baby and sit again with her during the night—with her and with the Lord in a tight circle of three." So try to look for the positives even when you're surrounded with negatives. It will lift your spirits and give you a desire to keep going.

FIGHTING LONELINESS

Mothers of young children are virtually never alone . . . not even in the bathroom. Actually, many of us have nursed babies while seated in there, and some of us have not only been feeding but also reading to a toddler sibling. Those moments of bathroom overcrowding make us long to have just a few minutes of alone time, yet one of the most common complaints young moms have is loneliness.

Toddler babble or baby cries can never satisfy your longing for real words in real conversations. As you work to raise your children, it's natural to feel isolated from all that's going on outside your four walls in the adult world. And when you're feeling lonely, a sure antidote is to spend time with close girlfriends.

Though conversation with a husband can meet a certain need for adult companionship, we all know they don't enjoy chatting as much as we do, not to mention they've never been moms. After an especially draining day, I (Mary) couldn't wait for my husband to walk through the door after work. His sympathizing ear would soothe my intense frustration and encourage me.

As soon as he was within earshot, I began detailing my distressing day, eager for his encouragement. When he reminded me I was blessed to be a mother and ought not to be complaining as I was, it didn't do a thing to help me. Since he was unwilling to give credence to my complaints, I snatched a piece of notebook paper from a nearby table and wrote, "I UNDERSTAND!" in big, bold, capital letters.

Then I held the paper in front of his face and said, "Say this to me."

He did, and though I knew he didn't really understand, it helped a little. But better than expecting your husband to sympathize with the relentless demands of motherhood, it's more effective to find another mother.

When the two of us were at-home moms to newborns and several toddlers, we made the life-altering decision to join forces and address some of the problems of isolation. Fortunately we lived only four miles apart. If you don't have a nearby sister, a close friend will work just as well.

One day each week we decided to pool our children. One of us would care for all of them while the other had free time. This arrangement went from 9:00 a.m. to 3:00 p.m. or so. The free mom could run errands, visit her doctor, or stay home with a good book. As for the one who was chasing after five or six little ones, no matter how hectic it got, she knew her free day was coming.

We christened these life-saving arrangements "Trade Days," but the reason they helped mama-loneliness came at the end of them. When the "free" mom returned to collect her children, we'd always brew some fresh coffee and settle in for a long, revitalizing chat. It was a time to catch up as girlfriends, share news, or ask advice. We could laugh together over silly things the children did, which is far more fun than laughing by yourself. And we could talk seriously, detailing problems and hashing out solutions.

But what if you don't have a girlfriend-mom? You know she's out there somewhere, experiencing the same loneliness you are, but how do you find her?

Both of us have met our dearest friends in church nurseries. It comes naturally to get acquainted while feeding babies in a nursery's back room or behind a partition. Just being together in that intimate setting assures these women have much in common. Moms who have older children can advise those adjusting to their first babies, and it's not uncommon for mentoring relationships to develop.

Bonding with women in church led to signing up for nursery duty, which then led to serving on the nursery's management committee. As we worked shoulder to shoulder with other moms, we had fun caring for other people's children as well as our own, and strong friendships quickly developed. After four decades, those same friendships are still going strong.

But church nurseries aren't the only places to connect with other mothers. As you visit local parks and playgrounds, kiddies in tow, watch for moms who are pushing strollers, changing diapers on park benches, or passing out sippy cups. More than likely they're craving adult conversation as much as you are. As the two of you stand side by side pushing swings, a friendship can be born with little effort.

WHERE TO FIND ANOTHER MOTHER

- Church nurseries
- Parks
- Book clubs
- Co-ops
- Neighborhoods
- Bible studies
- Health clubs
- Relatives
- MOPS meetings
- Sunday school classes

The same is true in your neighborhood. Make it a point to get out and about whenever the weather allows. Even if you don't succeed in finding a friend right away, the effort is always worth it. Fresh air and a change of scene does wonders for a lonely mom, and exchanging smiles with others delivers a mini boost.

If you find you just can't get out, the internet offers chat rooms for moms who share the same concerns or struggles. Taking a few minutes to dive into a topic of interest can result in cyberfriendships that carry through different ages and stages of raising children. You'll also learn how other moms do things and can put their experience to use, making your life a bit easier.

One thing both of us avoided during lonely periods was turning on the TV. Devoting too much time to Hollywood can tie you to a world of fantasy that makes you long to be someone you're not. You can easily get hooked on certain shows and fall into the trap of thinking everyone else's life is better than yours. Reality TV is the worst. It can fill your home with angry voices and discord, not to mention a never-ending string of bleeped words. Worst of all, these shows can convince you that devoting yourself to your family is second (or third or fourth) best.

GUIDELINES FOR TRADE DAYS

- Trade each week.
- Trade with a mom you trust.
- Trade for several hours.
- Trade equal number of children.
- Trade expecting to work hard

  or

- Trade expecting to be free!

Whenever you're struggling with loneliness, remind yourself that your children are priceless gifts from God, and He is highly invested in your efforts as a mother. He stands ready to help meet your needs, whatever they are. All you have to do is speak to Him, tell Him what you'd like help with, and He'll deliver it.

Once in a while He'll even meet a need through the children who are making you feel isolated. I (Margaret) remember a time when my fourth and fifth babies were ages one and two. As I reached into the dryer to pull out clean laundry, they stuffed it back in. If I folded a shirt, they snatched it off the pile and shook it out. When I wasn't watching, one of them would climb inside the dryer and sit on the clothes.

None of this was earth shattering, but not being able to do my work that day put me over my tipping point, and I lost it. Out loud, through sobs, I said, "Lord! It's not like I'm asking to read a magazine or take a bubble bath! I'm just trying to fold laundry!"

My two-year-old sensed trouble and immediately wrapped his pudgy little arms around my leg. "Lubb-ooo," he said in a soothing tone, looking up at me. He tried to comfort his mother the only way he knew how. It worked, and I could smile at him through my tears.

For all I knew, it was the Holy Spirit himself who spoke through little Klaus that day, because his "lubb-ooo" was so effective. God knew my need and met it well.

Let God know what you want Him to do for you, and He'll help you in some very creative ways.

Fighting Accumulation

We have watched TV shows where crews step into homes whose owners have let possessions run amok. These people allowed accumulation to grow into disarray, which then grew into dysfunction, forcing families to surrender dreams while just trying to survive.

It's easy for young moms to feel their possessions will take over their lives, especially when a new baby enters the scene. We need to set boundaries for what we'll let ourselves accumulate.

Before buying a new piece of baby equipment, consider becoming a borrower. Which friend is three years ahead of you in motherhood and would be happy to loan an infant car seat or a Pack 'n' Play? As a thank-you, invite her to lunch or watch her child while she shops. Make her so happy she'll ask you what else you need. "Here, take my infant bathtub. How about my baby carrier?"

Make a list of everything you'll need and then, after exhausting your borrowing options, consider renting. Call your community center and local hospital. An expensive item like a breast pump can often be rented for a nominal fee as long as you bring it back in good condition. Some communities have borrowing services for baby gates, high chairs, and other equipment.

If you want to own those items for future children, browse through consignment shops. When all of your children outgrow a piece of equipment, see if you can sell the high chair, baby gate, or other equipment back. And of course there are garage sales and internet options: Craig's list, eBay, FreeCycle, and Buy Nothing groups that are springing up in many neighborhoods.

SHOULD I BORROW, BUY, OR RENT?

- How long will I need this item?
- How expensive is this item to buy?
- How will I store this item?
- How quickly will this be outdated?
- How much stuff does my child need?

Babies fly through their early stages quickly; some items are barely used before it's time to upgrade. Consider a bouncy seat, which is no longer practical after a child learns to sit. Even swings come in infant sizes and bigger-baby models, neither used very long.

If you do decide to buy, think long term. Which items fold up or dismantle? Which brand will be durable enough for several children? What might I want to store for grandchildren someday?

And while you're thinking of storage space, what else might be valuable to keep? What about your child's medical records? Maybe a baby book or box? How about hard-copy photos? A lock of hair? Christening gown? Baby's first shoes? If we try to save everything, we might end up on that show about hoarding. So what is important to keep?

Pediatricians keep detailed records on every child they see, noting dates, ages, weights, what kind of exam they conducted, symptoms of illnesses, impressions of the visit and what medicines, vaccines, or treatments they did or recommended. As difficult as it is, we ought to keep similar records at home.

Throughout your child's life you'll need to refer to this information again and again. But how can you remember what happened on any one doctor visit? If you're juggling a frightened toddler and a screaming infant, it's difficult to keep a level head, much less remember what the doctor says.

I (Margaret) often asked our doctor to jot down what he did to (or for) each child. Who got the shots that day? Which ones? What was I to do if she got a fever that night? What did he recommend for chronic earaches or constipation?

My (Mary's) pediatrician handed out data booklets similar to checkbooks when a child became a new patient. That made it easy to keep track of physical exams. And by the way, when our doctor retired, I made sure to request our medical records before she left her practice.

These days it's easy to record data on your computer, backing it up so it never disappears. After that, when your child begins school or heads for summer camp, it'll be easy to fill in the blanks that ask for the date of his last tetanus shot or TB test.

What other items are important to save? A child's birth certificate, of course, and social security card. You will need both on countless occasions through his childhood and into adulthood. But what about sentimental items?

I (Margaret) was so enamored with our first child that I wanted to save everything he touched. When he went to preschool, I filed every shred of artwork—even if it was meaningless scribbles—and after real school began, I could see evidence of hoarding too much of a good thing.

In the end I boiled it down to a baby book and one large plastic bin of things special to him and us, like that first pair of shoes. You might want to skip the baby book and use a sturdy shoe box or even an accordion folder instead. Some moms focus on picture books assembled online through sites like Shutterfly or Snapfish, taking pictures of chunky things like baby shoes without having to save the shoes themselves. A thirty-page picture book fits nicely on a sliver of bookshelf space while a plastic bin can become a storage problem. I also made a small journal for each of our children by taking a picture in the same spot each month the first year. (Some people do it annually, throughout childhood.) Then I wrote a summary of what developments occurred during that month, ending up with a twenty-four-page synopsis of each child's first year.

I (Mary) saved each child's going-home-from-the-hospital outfit, baby blankets, special toys, special T-shirts, plaster handprints, and pictures of important events. In the beginning, I saved everything, but eventually that got out of control. So I chose a plastic bin, one for each child, and added items I couldn't bear to throw away. If the bin was full when I went to add something new, I had to remove something else. I'm glad I saved these special treasures of childhood. As I bring them out here and there, our adult children really enjoy them.

Some moms like to keep a baby book and record such things as a child's speech development, including first sounds and first words. Others write up the birth story—something children never tire of hearing—or their first impressions of motherhood. Making a family tree is also valuable, preserving the names and birth dates of older generations no one knows but you. I (Margaret) have gift wrapped many of these "saves" to give to my adult children on their birthdays—always a big hit.

THE BEST BABY BOX

- Detailed birth story
- Family tree
- First impressions
- Lock of baby's hair
- Dedication/baptism/ christening certificate
- Baby's favorite toy or blanket
- Monthly photo of baby's first year
- Handprints, plaster or otherwise
- Baby shoes or special outfits

As we're able to show our children what we saved from their babyhoods, it's one more way to tell them how much we love them and that we always have, right from the beginning.

So as you wonder how you'll ever keep all your plates spinning with the expertise of a circus performer, keep in mind that the One who gave you the task of mothering is the same One who's ready to fortify you to do everything that must be done.

Strengthen the feeble hands, steady the knees that give way;
say to those with fearful hearts . . . your God will come.
Isaiah 35:3–4

What can you do today?

Tidy up a drawer or a closet shelf, any one thing that will last more than twenty-four hours. When you need a lift, admire what you accomplished.

We wish we'd known . . .
1. mothering is never-ending hard work.
2. mothers have a unique place in God's heart.
3. motherhood is easier when shared with other mothers.

Chapter 5

LET THEM EAT SOAP!

God . . . will not forget your work
and the love you have shown him
as you have helped his people and continue to help them.
Hebrews 6:10

"Mom! Weezi cut all her hair off!"

Our family of nine (Margaret's) was in the final hours of preparing to leave on a month's vacation in northern Wisconsin. I'd been packing for two weeks, trying to remember everything from towels to toys to TP. Our children, ages two to nineteen, were going to need an endless variety of supplies.

On this last day we had hoped to start the seven-hour drive by midmorning, but it was already 1:00 p.m. and we weren't even close. When eleven-year-old Klaus came running with the news of four-year-old Louisa's haircutting, I still had lots more items to check off my long list.

Yanking myself from giant piles of stuff, I followed Klaus to our next-door-neighbor's yard where Louisa and her pal Sam, also four, were rounding the corner. Each had scissors in hand, and Weezi's long ponytail was completely missing—a one-inch, brushlike stump in its place. Her bangs no longer had a center section, and there were several bare spots around the perimeter of her head. Sam, too, had chopped some hair, but his many curls camouflaged the damage.

"Weezi!" I said, taking the scissors. "*What* did you do?" Not that I needed an answer.

No Perfect Mother

Surprised by the alarm on my face, she said, "We were just cutting the grass, Mommy, and the scissors got in our hair."

I grabbed her wrist and marched her toward the house, a spanking on my mind. "You know the rules!" I said. "No haircutting!"

Not pausing long enough to let her respond, I said, "When you cut your Barbie's hair, I told you that. You know better!"

She was crying before we reached the bathroom, and after I spanked her, I took her on my lap to restore our relationship. But my heart wasn't in it. I was still angry. She had added a new burden to an already bogged-down day.

But God was with us in the bathroom and immediately made His presence known. In my spirit I heard Him ask, "Are you absolutely sure she knew it was wrong to cut her hair? Or was it just innocent experimenting? And by the way, you *know* what I think of spanking in anger."

These thoughts brought me up short, and of course He was right. As the truth sank in, I began to feel awful. Though my day hadn't been going well, it was unfair to take it out on Louisa. And I racked my brain to recall the moment I'd told her never to cut her hair. Though I had chided her for butchering her Barbie doll, I couldn't remember if I'd translated that to human hair.

As Weezi sat whimpering on my lap, I was being disciplined by God. I had committed three serious offenses: spanking in anger, punishing for a vague reason, and damaging the relationship with my little girl.

Feeling sorry, I decided to call a nearby salon to see if we could minimize the damage with a professional haircut. As my wounded daughter sat in the beautician's chair, she looked into the mirror in front of her . . . at me. Our gazes locked, and I saw her eyes brim with new tears. It would take a long time to repair the harm I'd caused.

> ## When Your Child Pushes Your Hot Button
>
> - Take a deep breath.
> - Refuse the urge to react.
> - Pray quickly.
> - Keep a calm demeanor.
> - Isolate your child.
> - Leave the room if you must.

Back at home I returned to my packing piles, and our caravan of cars plus trailer pulled into the resort close to 3:00 a.m., a rocky start to a family vacation. Poor Louisa felt as ragged as she looked until I finally took her aside and admitted I'd been wrong. I told her why I felt that way and expressed sadness over my actions. When I asked her to forgive me, she did so immediately, giving lavish grace to a mother who had given her none at all.

Perfect Consequences

Disciplining children can be the most difficult part of parenting, and parents don't automatically know how best to handle infractions without overdoing or underdoing. It's tricky to hit it just right, since each child is different and each "crime scene" is unique.

That doesn't let mothers off the hook, though. The Bible is replete with examples of what happens when children are left to discipline themselves before they're old enough to know how. And Scripture gives plenty of info on how to do it right. The old idea, "Spare the rod and spoil the child" actually originates with God (Proverbs 22:15). But even after we've nodded in agreement, we often find ourselves in blurry situations.

Both of us have learned through our mistakes that the best way to discipline is to let natural consequences do it for you. I (Mary) remember my first experience with this and how well it worked. Julia was barely two years old, playing in the bathtub one day, when she repeatedly grabbed a bar of pink soap from the built-in soap dish. She badly wanted to take a bite, and I knew she needed to learn soap wasn't for eating.

"No-no," I said again and again, taking the soap from her and putting it back. "Yucky. We don't eat soap."

With typical toddler persistence, she continued to reach for it, and I knew I'd have to press my point. Either I'd have to remove the soap, despite my wanting it to stay there, or I'd have to slap her hand, which I was reluctant to do. Without one of the two, our soap battle would continue indefinitely—that is, until I realized I had one more option. I could let her eat the soap.

Leaning back, I watched her grab it, take a bite, make a face, and put it back. She never reached for it again. Done.

Julia's behavior was simply childish curiosity. At her age it was difficult to take my word for anything, and allowing natural consequences to teach the lesson was quick, easy, and (I believe) superior to slapping her or continually removing the soap.

Children learn about gravity by falling off of things, about the meaning of "hot" with a finger-touch on something hot, and about water by splashing it up their noses. Shielding them from these natural consequences is like shooting yourself in the foot. Not only will it take much longer for them to learn by other means, it'll also increase your workload. Of course, you're not going to let them run into a busy street to learn about traffic, but whenever possible, let experience be their teacher.

Some young moms object to this kind of natural learning because they don't ever want to cause distress in their children. Neither of us did well at allowing our little ones to cry, but we both learned that keeping children content every minute isn't a good philosophy either. It promotes the lie that they are the center of their world as well as ours, and everyone else is on the periphery. It's just a short hop from there to, "I'm better than you are."

The other option is to babyproof your house so thoroughly you no longer want to live there. If you make a child's world devoid of the natural consequences, how will he learn? Actions always speak louder than words, especially their *own* actions. Besides, childproofing your home can become a subtle trap for parents too.

Wanting to protect them from all harm can lead to overprotecting. That, then, can lead to usurping decisions young children ought to make for themselves. It's true that your decisions *for* them will always be the safer ones, but if you eliminate all the natural consequences, you're setting the stage for micromanaging the rest of their childhood years . . . right up till they leave for college. Your motto may have been "safety first" all along, but once they're out of your nest, making all their own decisions at last, some very important lessons may not have been learned.

When Louisa hacked off her hair, I should have let natural consequences be her teacher. Without the misery of a spanking, she would have learned that cutting her own hair didn't result in a good look. A second lesson could have been that hair grows very slowly, and her choppy look was going to last a long time. She'd loved her ponytail, and now it was gone.

One final note: as an adult, Louisa chose to attend beauty school to learn to cut hair, and these days she does all the haircutting for our entire extended family. Even me.

PERFECT LOVE

Mother-love has been called the greatest power on earth, and most of us wouldn't think twice about jumping in front of a car to save our children. As a mom, you may be taken aback by the magnitude of love you feel for your little ones. And loving them that passionately makes you want to provide them with peaceful, secure, happy, safe lives. It's a shock to discover the best way to accomplish that is to limit them.

Although children would never admit it, they long for parents to set boundaries, instinctively knowing that this is what love does. Giving kids all kinds of freedom sounds like the route to happiness, but just the opposite is true. The decisions they make as children will always lack wisdom, because they haven't lived long enough to acquire any. But worse than that, receiving too much freedom too soon usually leads to chaos, insecurity, unhappiness, and danger—the opposite of what you want for them.

Children who run their own lives at young ages consistently make foolish (childish) decisions, resulting in behavioral extremes that make it unpleasant to be around them. They don't listen to reason, and without exception they put themselves first.

The Bible says, "A child left to himself brings shame to his mother" (Proverbs 29:15 ESV). No mom wants that. Thankfully, Scripture details exactly how to successfully raise children, starting with the powerful reassurance that God wants to be part of the project.

So when you're faced with a belligerent child whose strongest desire is to take control away from you (control of the moment, the family, the household, the schedule), step forward in parental strength against that. The Lord will back you up with His power as you follow His instructions. There will be loud objections and plenty of pushback, maybe even full-blown tantrums. But with the determination God gives you, coupled with His ideas, you can (and must) prevail.

PERFECT INSTRUCTION

> ### TIPS FOR TANTRUMS
>
> - Isolate the offender.
> - Don't try to reason with him.
> - Quietly model self-control.
> - Ignore him.
> - Spritz him with cool water.
> - Praise a child who controls himself.

God's instruction on disciplining children is for parents to focus on training rather than punishing. In other words, it shouldn't always be about catching a child in the wrong and dishing out a penalty as much as it is about coaching them to learn new skills and develop godly character. Of course, some things are more difficult to learn than others, necessitating greater patience over a longer period of time on the part of the instructor.

For example, training a child in proper teeth brushing is far easier than teaching him to be kind. Demonstrating how to eat with a fork goes quicker than coaching a child to share. No matter the goal, parents should remember that their child is in training. Mistakes are inevitable, just as they are for adults who struggle to learn something new.

God, as our heavenly Father, exercises endless patience in His training regimens, giving us second, third, and fourth chances to learn the same lessons. Often, He'll use natural consequences as His teaching tool rather than bringing down the hammer when we fail. He lets us try again and again, always having our best interests at heart.

Sometimes we obstinately tell Him we don't want to learn what He's teaching, but even then, He remains loving, hopeful we'll eventually come around to wanting His wise will. Usually, though, He doesn't force us. Instead, He waits to see if we'll cooperate with Him on our own. Because we are His children, He never gives up expecting the best of us.

Of course a young mom can't always respond to the resistance of children the way God responds to us. Everyday life leaves very little waiting time, and you can become highly frustrated when training efforts are met with opposition. If that happens and tension is high, it might be best to break stride with what's going on. This might even be the reason God tells us to "give thanks in all circumstances" (1 Thessalonians 5:18).

Is there something in the middle of that frustrating moment you can thank God for? With an irritated (and irritating) child standing in front of you, gratitude goes against logic, but God's logic isn't like ours. If you breathe a prayer asking what to be thankful for, He might even give you something new to appreciate about that particular child.

```
Training Tools to Use

•   A fun challenge
•   Complimentary words
•   Rewards
•   Punishment
•   Gentle reprimand
```

Another thing you might try as both you and she are spiraling downward is to praise or compliment—more nonlogic from God. Words of praise often lead children to respond exactly as you want them to, working even better than punishment. Proverbs 16:21 says, "The wise are known for their understanding, and pleasant words are persuasive." What positive words might you say to her that she may find persuasive?

For example, if you tell your five-year-old to keep an eye on your two-year-old for a minute while you run to the bathroom, and if she objects you might say, "Honey, you are always so good with little children and have such talent for entertaining them," or "Sweetie, your little brother looks up to you and loves spending time with you. He thinks you're the greatest!" Pleasant words can be persuasive, so use them as a tool to accomplish your goals.

Other pleasant words that might persuade are, "If you help Mommy get her work done by watching your little brother, we'll have time to walk around the block together." Additional rewards for cooperation could be playing with certain toys that are usually put away or getting a sweet treat. Some children also respond well to a challenge: "While Mommy runs upstairs to get something, see how high you can count before I get back."

If resistance continues, of course you have to try another approach and might end up disciplining the offender for disobedience. But always keep in mind that any discipline you use must be administered with a desire to train. Never let your own frustration make you choose the wrong penalty. A child shouldn't have to suffer consequences not linked to the crime, since the result would be confusion and hurt rather than learning.

Never Discipline when You Are . . .

- in front of others
- angry at your child
- motivated by peer pressure
- unsure of guilt
- frustrated by the situation
- embarrassed by your child
- in a hurry

On those occasions when a child willfully defies a parent, however, an appropriate penalty is in order. But be careful. If you punish too harshly, the fallout may include your child becoming deeply discouraged or even fearful of you. Though no one enjoys being disciplined (Hebrews 12:11), when it's done thoughtfully, patiently, and in love, it makes sense to a child and will ultimately produce good fruit. God promises that.

So when you're confused about how to handle a prickly situation, approach the Master-Trainer for advice. He'll tell you what to do by planting practical (and perfect) ideas in your head. If you follow His recommendations, you can be sure you've done the most loving thing for your child. And because of that, you can expect the positive results God describes.

In a biblical list of good parenting qualities (compassion, kindness, humility, meekness, patience, forgiveness), love is labeled as being above them all. "Above all these put on love, which binds everything together in perfect harmony" (Colossians 3:14 ESV). As you discipline your errant children, work at doing so from a heart of love. When you do, your family will have a good shot at perfect harmony . . . because, once again, God says so.

PERFECT CHILD?

Maybe you entered motherhood believing that since you studied what the experts said and then planned to heed their advice, you would raise a nearly perfect child. Since that hasn't happened, you've become irritated with the experts and resentful toward your youngster.

It's definitely upsetting that children don't always respond correctly to your well-meaning attempts at loving discipline. But before you despair, ask yourself two critical questions:

(1) Was the crime out-and-out disobedience or just natural childishness?

(2) Is it possible the whole thing was my fault?

How do you determine whether a youngster blundered by accident or on purpose? Young children are clumsy and uncoordinated. We've seen our kids walk into door frames while looking straight at them and fall to the ground after stumbling over nothing. So when they knock over their milk at a meal or splash water on the floor during bath time, is it willful disobedience or just ordinary childishness? The answer ought to determine how you respond.

Remember that the goal is to train them, though that doesn't mean pressuring them to act like mini adults. Regardless of the magnitude of the mess or inconvenience, the most important thing is to determine how the situation happened and to ask, *Is there a need behind the deed?* In other words, what is the motive behind the action? Where is your child's heart?

Of course a child can knock over milk or soak the bathroom floor with rebellious intent, but one surefire way to tell the difference is to watch his face. If he seems surprised by your objections, you know it was unintended and should be covered with grace. If he begins making excuses, it was probably deliberate and needs to be dealt with accordingly.

As to the second question, whether or not a mom is to blame, I (Mary) have a sad parenting memory that started with a picture-perfect scene. My husband was standing at the bathroom sink shaving while two-year-old Luke mirrored his movements with his own bladeless razor. Knowing five-month-old Julia would enjoy watching them both, I buckled her into her plastic infant seat (in those days a narrow, laid-back chair with a flimsy wire base) and set her on the counter.

Within a few minutes of leaving the bathroom I heard screams and rushed back to find my husband lifting Julia off the floor. "What happened?" I said with alarm.

"She went over the side!" my husband said, dismayed by his daughter's wailing.

Little Luke, concentrating on the mirror and his shaving, had nudged Julia's infant seat just an inch or two, enough to send it sailing. And I knew immediately the accident wasn't his fault but mine. The countertop was narrow, and I should have thought twice about placing her so close to the edge. I also knew better than to rely on a two-year-old to be conscious of a baby's safety.

Often when something like this goes wrong, we quickly look for someone to blame. *Who's responsible? Who's going to pay?* Though it was Luke who nudged her off, it was me who was responsible—actually, irresponsible. Owning up to it was difficult, since it meant I was the cause of my baby's black eye. To makes matters worse, I knew it could have easily been prevented.

That day I didn't reprimand Luke, though on other occasions I did discipline wrongly. But punishing before analyzing is a temptation for every mom. Sadly, if we dish out discipline for a crime that was simply childishness or if we blame a child for what was a mother's fault, it's our little ones who suffer. And when children suffer needlessly, their mothers suffer too.

> ### Nonnegotiable Offenses
>
> - Defying authority
> - Hurting another child
> - Disrespecting any adult

One thing is sure, though. When moms are moving through a day that has no wiggle room in it and a young child causes a crisis that forces a slowdown, moms are more likely to make the wrong call. Though we do so unwittingly, the result can be a serious wounding of a young heart. Recently I (Margaret) talked with my adult Louisa about the haircut incident that happened over twenty years ago. I'd made a wrong call on that miserable day, spanking her for something that was mere childish curiosity. And she hadn't forgotten.

"How did you feel after I spanked you that day?" I said.

"I thought you hated me."

Even though I'd long since shared my regrets with her and told her how sorry I was, and even though she'd forgiven me ages ago, her statement made me sad all over again. Improper discipline is no respecter of persons and distributes heartache all around. So be sure to take the needed time to check the details, become aware of your child's motives, and take an honest look at your own. This should all be done before you respond.

A good guideline is to copy what God does. Before disciplining, He looks at our hearts (1 Samuel 16:7). Mothers ought to do the same. Though we can't always analyze correctly or act with perfection, we can steadily improve.

PERFECT PROBLEM-SOLVING

Motherhood presents all sorts of practical dilemmas. There are eating issues, bedtime battles, toilet training disputes, and so much more. In deciding whether to discipline a child, first think ahead to the way each struggle might go and decide if it's worth it. Is there a chance you're making a mountain out of a molehill? If so, let it pass. Also, ask yourself if you have the time to deal with it properly right then. If you're in a rush, tackle it later. And be sure that if you decide to get into it, it's a battle you can actually win. There *are* some you can't.

Take eating, for example. No matter how you coax, bribe, or penalize, you can't make a child swallow food. One of ours walked around with a bite of food in her mouth for hours, unwilling to swallow. Unless you force a feeding tube (ridiculous), you can't make them eat what you want, when you want.

I (Mary) learned about eating issues with one-year-old Marta. As a baby, then a toddler, she was a picky eater to the max. She didn't have an ounce of fat on her because she refused to eat 90 percent of whatever I cooked. Though I tried every trick in the book to make food appealing to her, she just wouldn't eat. Gut instinct told me it would be wrong to discipline her for lack of an appetite, especially since she was a sweet, compliant child in every other respect. But I didn't know what to do.

Every Saturday morning I made Swedish pancakes for our family, and little Marta was willing to eat one of those. So I decided to make it my mission to produce Swedish pancakes every day of the week, just for her—breakfast, lunch, and dinner. Because she needed calories, I substituted cream for the milk and went heavy on the eggs. It didn't bother me that she wanted to dip her pancakes into a puddle of syrup. Anything to get her to eat.

She ate pancakes every day during those many months, and eventually she began tasting other things too. Had I punished her for refusing to eat, I don't believe it would have helped in any way. It certainly would have made her dread family mealtimes and probably would have damaged our relationship. Today Marta is a healthy twenty-six-year-old with a normal appetite. And though she eats virtually all foods, she has a special fondness for Swedish pancakes.

Some moms say you shouldn't "go with your gut," but we believe a mother's instincts are God-given. At a bare minimum, when you feel like things aren't quite right or that something about the situation or your child is slightly off, wait for clarity. Listen to your instincts, and go with your gut.

How *Not* to Have Whine with Every Meal

- Set attainable goals for meals.
- Serve foods your child likes.
- Dish up child-size portions.
- Keep mealtimes short and sweet.
- Encourage new foods without forcing.
- Praise a willingness to try new foods.
- Expect childlike behavior from your child.
- Never allow a whiner to ruin mealtime.

Another mothering war zone can be sleeping habits. Short of medicating your child into unconsciousness (please don't!), nothing you do will ensure he'll sleep when you want, for as long as you want. But bedtime should not be characterized by strife and anxiety. Keep a high standard for the last minutes of your child's day, knowing that whatever happens then will be on his mind as he drifts into sleep. And it may still be there first thing in the morning.

Most young children are reluctant to end the day when it's time to head for bed. Not only does it initiate isolation from other family members, it signifies putting toys away and ending playtime. That's why children work to keep mommy in the room as long as possible. Unbeknownst to them, however, this strategy on their part becomes a powerful perk for mothers who want to take advantage of this tender time.

Your youngsters become especially warm to what you do during these moments, hanging on your every word. It becomes an optimal time to memorize a short line of Scripture or sing a song. I (Margaret) sang bedtime choruses to Nelson, our firstborn, starting when he was about a year old. As he learned to talk, he picked up the words, and by the time he was three, he had memorized (and could sing) fifty-five Sunday school songs.

These short choruses were full of God's truth, simplified for children, and as the two of us continued singing, Nelson often asked questions about the words, attentive to my answers.

Be sure to include a prayer of blessing over your child before you leave the room. God is there listening to you and loves to answer a mother's heartfelt prayers.

These bedtime suggestions might sound elaborate and time consuming, but the whole thing can be done in just a few minutes. Think of it as the most valuable part of your routine, even more important than having a bath or brushing teeth.

As you step out of the room, along with your "night-night, honey," conclude this time with something uplifting. "I love you very much, darling," or "See you in the morning!" Staying positive is better than, "I hope you'll do better tomorrow." Try to express unconditional love . . . one more time.

Another area that can quickly move to battle status is toilet training. Think carefully before you get started. Never move ahead just because the calendar or other mothers say you should unless you want to live in the bathroom for long stretches while holding her on the potty. We learned to wait until our children were literally begging to wear "big-kid pants" before taking them out of diapers. If you put them off long enough, they'll be promising *you* rewards if you'll just pleeeease let them pee in the potty.

TAKE THE TERROR OUT OF TOILET TRAINING

- Refuse to let peer pressure influence.
- Wait till your child shows interest.
- Stay positive, at least on the outside.
- Don't let it become a power struggle.
- Never belittle or punish failure.
- Reward every small success.
- Be your child's cheerleader.

Many of these childhood crises will take care of themselves if you wait long enough. All children eventually learn to enjoy food, sleep when put to bed, and wear pants instead of diapers. Remember, every battle you lose is a big step backward.

PERFECT WISDOM

I (Margaret) remember a day that had not been going well. I was feeling overworked, underappreciated, and tired of the daily grind. Changing nine-month-old Hans' diaper for the fourth time that day, I began slipping into a funk. My life didn't seem to count for much. It's a wonder I didn't get a lightning bolt to the head, seeing as it was so swollen with self-centeredness.

Instead God planted a couple of potent thoughts: *Hans is My child, and the work you're doing is not as much for him as it is for Me. I see you there and am aware of your discouragement. But I'm thankful you're willing to be his mother. Please do it for Me.*

Zap—a lightning bolt after all. In one quick flash, God corrected my perspective, reminding me that being a mom was a high calling from Him. Everything I did as a mother was done indirectly for my child but directly for my Lord. Mothering wasn't a string of repetitive, mundane chores but rather acts of servanthood that could be dedicated to God.

Though it's true a mother's work is never done, that shouldn't be the banner superimposed over your calling as a mom. Knowing where you fit in the grand scheme of things can revolutionize every minute of every day. Mothering the specific children sent to you by God can then become one of life's greatest pleasures . . . even when changing your thousandth diaper.

It's easy to feel sorry for ourselves, especially when we're stretched to the limit. And it doesn't help that today's mothers are not lifted up and encouraged by society as they were in generations past. Moms who forfeit careers to stay home with their children are especially snubbed, but they ought never to base their opinion of themselves on what the culture says.

Followers of Christ find their identity in Him, the One who doesn't change through the generations. Every Christian mother ought to define her value as Scripture defines it, which is to take her worth from what the Lord says. After He made the first man and woman, His assessment of all He created went from *good* to *very good* (Genesis 1:31).

He's made each of us—including you—with the same great care and ascribes the same great value to each of us, since we're all made in His image. He breathed an eternal soul into you, and by Christ's death, has made a way to save that soul. He's offered to live within you to guide, encourage, help, and affirm you as needed. In other words, He wants to be your God on a personal level, one-on-one. Knowing all this should give you the strong confidence that you are of great worth.

And there's something else. He's given you children to raise, specific work to do in specific ways, and He daily offers to equip you for the task. The Lord highly esteems children, which is why raising them is important work. Though today's world might demean the role of mothering, God doesn't ever want you to feel demeaned as you do it.

So while working hard at this assignment, carefully evaluate the popular trends of the day, setting aside any that are contrary to your God-given intuition. If anyone criticizes you for the importance you place on motherhood, take your cues from the Lord, not them. As a matter of fact, if you raise your children as He instructs, you can be confident He's going to reward you big-time.

If you find yourself discouraged by the long-term, difficult nature of the job, you'll relate to this verse: "My work seems so useless! I have spent my strength for nothing and to no purpose. Yet I leave it all in the LORD's HAND; I WILL TRUST GOD FOR

MY REWARD" (ISAIAH 49:4 NLT). Trust God, knowing He will reward your work if you remain faithful in your mothering. No matter what anyone else says, lean into what God says instead.

When I was changing Hans' diaper, again, I had been defining myself by my feelings. Because they were all negative, I ascribed a negative definition to my job as a mom. This was a leap I should never have made, and thankfully God brought me back to His rich, reassuring truth that day.

UNCONDITIONAL LOVE FOR MOMS

- Spend three minutes reading Scripture.
- Buy a puppy.
- Write out a favorite verse or phrase.
- Remember the importance of raising children.
- Recall how much God loves you.
- Have another baby!

Finding your identity in Christ frees you from comparing yourself to other mothers or feeling like you need to compete with them. Because children are gifts from God, you can grasp the significance of what you do every day by recognizing that He had this exact job with these exact children in His plan for you long ago, well before you were born. The Bible says, "We are his workmanship created in Christ Jesus for good works, which God prepared beforehand, that we should walk in them" (Ephesians 2:10 ESV).

What you're doing every day is good work in God's mind. You're following through with what He prepared you to do, and by that you are bringing blessing to Him. The result will be that He blesses *you*! As you work at being the best mom you can be, remember that God is *for* you. And since that's true, no one else can prevail against you.

God wants you to succeed, and He wants your children to turn out well. So remind yourself—every hour of every day—that you belong to Him, just as your children do. He will never leave you hanging or fail to answer your call for help. Make sure you take advantage of that while you live out your calling as a mother, acknowledging that even the most distasteful chore can become meaningful when done for Him.

As you raise your children, don't let their training be draining. Remember that if you're faithful in your efforts, payday will eventually come. The Lord is watching you, cheering you on, appreciating your every effort. But He hopes you won't be content just to know He's watching. He greatly desires to be your helper too.

No discipline seems pleasant at the time, but painful.
Later on, however, it produces a harvest of righteousness
and peace for those who have been trained by it.
Hebrews 12:11

What can you do today?
Inspect a delicate flower, and realize how easily it can be crushed.

We wish we'd known . . .

1. that our children didn't always need to be kept happy.

2. that they would love and respect us more if we disciplined them.

3. to use fewer words and take more action.

Chapter 6

PEANUT BUTTER AND PEANUT BRITTLE BOTH TASTE GOOD

Thank you for making me so wonderfully complex!
Your workmanship is marvelous—how well I know it.
Psalm 139:14 NLT

One of the inaccurate assumptions I (Mary) made as a young mom was that I could raise my children in a little pack. Since they came from the same parents and were being raised in the same home with the same routine, I figured they'd all respond to me and my agenda in the same way. But God doesn't make cookie-cutter people.

How well I remember the small preschool we used for our first and second children. As the oldest, four-year-old Luke embraced every part of this first school experience. Two years later, Julia couldn't wait for her turn and happily walked into her classroom without looking back. And then came Karl.

It never occurred to me that since the first two responded positively to this childhood benchmark, the third would balk. All three of them had a neighborhood pal to partner with as they first went to school, but not even that convinced Karl to go happily. I thought that what was good for one would be good for all, but this child had none of the same bents as his older siblings. He was shy and sensitive, especially when away from home. And as the baby of the family during those years, he'd been pampered more than the others.

But I didn't focus on those differences. Instead, I ignored his daily objections and insisted he participate, some days literally dragging him to the car as he did everything in his power to change my mind.

Over weeks of time, Karl gradually accepted the reality that no amount of resistance was going to release him from his miserable preschool routine. He gave up trying and became passive, much like a child who finally submits to medicine he must take. And I insisted he attend the entire school year.

Looking back, forcing preschool was one of my mothering failures. Why did I feel so strongly about sending him against his will? After all, it was optional. One reason was that his older siblings had loved it. Another was that all the neighborhood moms were sending *their* four-year-olds, so I took my cue from them rather than from my own son. I had also bought into the trend of the day, which was to send little ones to preschool so they would "better fit in to our rapidly changing society." We were told that if they had an institutional experience before "real" school, they'd be better prepared to cope, and I believed it.

And one last reason why I thought it would be good for Karl to attend preschool was that I was desperate for alone time at home. With three young children and another on the way, my efficiency as a homemaker had gone out the window. Regular time alone could help me catch up.

None of these influencers should have trumped the needs of my child. I wrongly bowed to peer pressure and believed the lie that my son needed a classroom experience more than extra time with his mommy. To this day, I regret that decision.

God Loves Variety

Children born into the same family have different physical appearances, so why isn't it obvious that their insides are different too? The desire of mothers to lump them together stems from a need to simplify very active lives. Logic says that what was good for the first should be good for the second.

But as moms study their newborns, it isn't long before differences emerge. The first baby might have been fussy, the second content. The first wakeful, the second sleepy. The first vocal, the next quiet. And suddenly the mothering job gets harder because what worked for one fails to work for the other.

That's the way it is when God is in charge. He's full of ideas and never runs out of ways to make people unique. We believe He puts divine thought into the creation of each person, plucking some characteristics from parents, some from grandparents, and some from out of nowhere. As He puts people together, it's probable He does so with great pleasure. It makes sense, then, that He hopes mothers will hunt for—and appreciate—the differences in the children He sends.

No one knows your child better than you do. And if you're able to slow down long enough to study him carefully, you'll understand why he responds to you and others as he does. Once you learn who he is at his core, you can effectively train up your child in the way he should go (Proverbs 22:6). In other words, you can nudge him in the direction God has already programmed him to shine. As you put thought and energy into how to do this, the Lord will bless you with practical ideas, since He faithfully reinforces those who follow His lead.

If you try to squeeze your square peg into a round hole, you'll find you have to work twice as hard on your kids than a mom who simply goes along with God's natural giftings within the child. Most adults have experienced the rich satisfaction of using their natural abilities. Rather than a drain, it's rewarding and often fun. Forcing ourselves to do something that doesn't come naturally is both exhausting and frustrating. Children will make strong progress when cheered in the right direction, and God gives moms the coveted position of providing the approval and applause our children need to learn and grow.

MOMS KNOW THE DIFFERENCE

In addition to encouraging a child to follow his natural giftings, there are still a number of things parents need to teach that don't follow anything natural, like sharing possessions, handling anger properly, being generous, understanding the perspective of someone else, looking for blessings, listening carefully, telling the truth, and so much more. We adults have trouble learning these same things, so why shouldn't children? But if a parent faithfully pursues these teachings, the result will be a child who grows up to have sterling character—something that will be important throughout his adult life.

CHARACTER TRAITS TO ENCOURAGE

- Honesty
- Kindness
- Cheerfulness
- Cooperation
- Sharing
- Patience
- Generosity

Here's an example. When my son Klaus (Margaret's) was still a preschooler, God handed me a golden opportunity to teach honesty—an opportunity I tossed aside. As I was checking out at the grocery store with a full cart and several of my other children, Klaus stood in front of the enticing candy rack conveniently placed at his level, eyeing the array of goodies. Without an understanding of who could and couldn't help themselves to those treats, he selected a Snickers bar for himself.

After I paid the bill, gathered my children, and began wrestling the cart across a potholed parking lot, I noticed Klaus's candy. "Where did you get that?" I said.

"At the store, Mama."

"But you can't just take things from the store without paying for them."

"But *you* paid, Mama."

"Not for your candy bar."

"Why not?"

A four-year-old couldn't possibly understand the complications of grocery shopping, but we were in a hurry, so I answered by saying, "I just didn't."

After I'd taken the Snickers bar away from him, we loaded the car and proceeded home. I saw Klaus's furrowed brow in my rearview mirror and knew he was confused about what had just happened. With the right words spoken at the right time, I could have *trained up my child in the way God wanted him to go.*

Klaus had already shown he was good with people and wasn't afraid to approach strangers for a conversation. I could have marched him back into the store and coaxed him into a short talk with the checkout girl that would have taught him about both honesty and stealing.

Later that day, I tried to regain the loss. Klaus and I reached for his spending jar atop the refrigerator and counted out several coins. Then the two of us drove back to the store with the Snickers bar and his money, chatting about the candy display on the way—what was free and what wasn't and why, and what the word "honest" meant, since he didn't know. After all, he was only four.

As we went through the checkout line to buy the candy bar, I encouraged Klaus to talk to the girl about it. Without a shred of shyness, he lifted his Snickers bar to show her, telling her how he'd taken it from the rack earlier. Then he said, "I wasn't honest."

She entered into the dialogue with patience, and the shoppers behind us smiled their approval, two of them complimenting Klaus on his truthfulness.

After putting his coins into the girl's hand, Klaus proudly walked out of the store with his candy. Though the Snickers tasted good, he also got a taste of what honesty was all about. Had he been a shy child without an inclination toward sociability, this experience would have been torture. I'd have been wrong to ask him to do it that way. But since he was naturally gregarious, the teaching plan worked well.

I (Mary) could tell almost from the womb that my children would be radically different from each other. Julia, my second-born, had a strong leaning toward nurturing. She gravitated toward babies while she was still a baby herself, and her first word was "be-be." She consistently wanted to interact with babies and touch them.

On her second birthday we gave her a life-sized baby doll, and she carefully mothered her "Connie" alongside me as I mothered the baby brother who joined our family when Julia was twenty-one months. When she outgrew playing with dolls, she put her Connie on a bedroom shelf where she remained. Julia went on to babysit for all five of her younger siblings, and I counted on her to help me care for them through her own childhood years. Eventually Julia's own daughters played with Connie, who had been carefully preserved during the twenty-year interim.

Julia's first official job during her teen years was as a summertime nanny for a pediatrician. Her nurturing ability took her through nursing school and later into full-time motherhood, foster parenting, and adoption. And it was all evident from her babyhood.

Knowing ahead of time that God wires our children in specific ways encourages us to look for what those qualities are. We can read all the parenting books we want, but no one knows your child like you do—except God. A tried-and-true book about the rules of good mothering can only go so far in its effectiveness on your child. Far more important is to partner with the Lord, who knows her inside out, upside down, backward and forward. God knows, and so do you.

AFFIRM THE DIFFERENCES

Once you've identified several ways your young child is preprogrammed to go, what's next? First you talk to God about it, thanking Him for the way He chose to create your child. Since your little one might be your polar opposite in natural giftings, it's also a good idea to ask God to teach you what's best for that youngster. He knows, and He'll tell you.

Secondly, as you see your preschooler even slightly moving in the direction of her wiring, lavish praise on her. Admire her work. I (Mary) knew early on that our sixth child, Stina, was going to be strong in organizational skills. If she walked past a kitchen drawer that wasn't completely closed, her pudgy little hands would reach up and gently push it in that last inch or two. If the pens in the drawer were helter-skelter, she'd line them up neatly. If the shoes by the door were in a heap, she'd arrange them in pairs. If the kitchen stools were a-jumble, she'd slide them into their proper places.

These things astounded me because Stina was still a toddler. But God would have said, "She's just doing what I programmed her to do." As I lavished praise on her, it was clear by her expression she felt good using her natural bent.

WORDS THAT AFFIRM YOUR CHILD

- You're really good at that!
- I like what you made.
- You are very special to me.
- Let's play together, whatever you choose.
- What careful work you do!
- You are a gift from God.
- Thank you for obeying quickly.
- You've been a big help to me today.
- I enjoy being with you.
- I love you!

I (Margaret) noticed early on that our Nelson was mechanically inclined. As a toddler he organized his Matchbox cars in neat rows on the basement toy shelf. After turning three, his favorite toy was a wooden board on which we'd attached a key lock, a hook-and-eye fastener, a sliding chain lock and other gadgets. As a four-year-old he could assemble a simple kite, and by five he was pleading with his grandpa to teach him how to pound a nail in straight. He was fascinated with how things worked and would rather take toys apart than play with them.

Nelson grew up watching repairmen fix things, and he worked to emulate them. Tools fascinated him, and when he got his first car, he pushed through endless frustrations to learn how engines worked. I remember the day I was in the kitchen when he came running in. "Mom! Come into the garage! I want to show you something amazing!" It was the universal joint in his old Jeep.

Make it your goal to identify your child's strengths and help them understand what they are. As you work together to develop these talents, you'll find yourself growing closer to that child in ways satisfying to you both.

Comparing Kids

Since no two children are alike, comparing is always apples to oranges. Yet all parents do it, and not always for the wrong reasons. For example, a mom may wonder if all is well with her child, worrying about something that doesn't seem right. One way she investigates is to compare.

"My baby doesn't make eye contact and seems to look away when I talk to her. Is this normal?" Comparing with other babies might alert her to a genuine problem. Except for rare exceptions like that, though, the only good reason to compare children is to spot their differences. If a mother fails to look closely at what her children can and cannot do, she's liable to lump them together in ways that become detrimental.

She might push them into the same sport, for example, expecting them to be equally enthusiastic and proficient, even if one or two aren't coordinated or sports-minded at all. Or she might insist on piano lessons all around, despite one being tone deaf and another having zero musical interest.

Comparing kids as you decide which classes, teams, or activities to register for can yield a helpful list of reasons why or why not. Second-borns, for instance, almost always follow a path different from their firstborn siblings. A wise mother understands this and doesn't attempt to make one childhood identical to another. If she insists on uniformity, at least one of her children isn't being accepted for who he really is.

RESULTS OF COMPARING

- Feelings of inferiority
- Unnecessary jealousy
- Deep emotional wounds
- A sense of being unloved
- Extra stress in mommy
- Denial of natural bents
- Aggression between children

Studying your children can be a complicated business. After noticing their different leanings, moms automatically compare them to each other. But remind yourself often that from God's perspective, each stands alone and no talent or gift makes one child superior to another. Even what appears to be a weakness can change into a strength in His hands.

One other caution: since logic says you'll view your children through your own innate talents, it's important not to elevate one child over another just because his bent matches yours. Though you may relate more naturally to that youngster, be careful you don't favor him without realizing it. Both the favored and the unfavored will eventually pick up on it, and the result will be anger and resentment—toward you and the sibling.

Ephesians 6:4 says, "Do not provoke your children to anger by the way you treat them" (NLT). In other words, if you treat them incorrectly, anger will be the inevitable result. The last half of the verse describes how to treat them well. "Rather, bring them up with the discipline and instruction that comes from the Lord."

As you learn all you can about how each of your children is wired, what different instructions do you think God has attached to them? Ask yourself, which activities would work best for her? What encouragement from you will validate the way she was made? What approach will partner with what God is already doing in her life? Raising children is a difficult job, and doing it one by one makes it more so. But your frustrations will be less and disappointments fewer if you follow God's lead.

If we attempt to raise children in a group, negative comparisons are inevitable. "Why can't you hear that your notes are off? Your brother never misses that" or "When will you learn to throw a ball right? Your sister does it so much better than you." These statements send damaging messages to children. What they hear is, "You don't measure up. You aren't as valuable as your sibling. You are a disappointment. You do things wrong."

What *Not* to Say to Your Child

- Why can't you be like your brother?
- You're a bad girl.
- You don't measure up.
- You're too big to wet your pants.
- There's nothing to be afraid of.
- Sometimes I don't like you.
- You aren't as valuable as your sister.
- I don't know what to do with you.
- You do things wrong.
- Just wait till your daddy gets home.
- I knew you would make a big mess.
- You are hard to love.
- You're a disappointment to me.
- I wish you'd never been born.

THOUGH THEY DIFFER, EXPECT THE BEST

Comparisons are the breeding ground for inferiority complexes. Though some children balk at pursuing what a mother insists they do, a compliant child who lives to please might pour everything she has into pursuing something she's not the least bit interested in. From this she learns it's OK to do things for the wrong reasons, and it's very possible she'll become a pleaser in areas she ought not to be.

Ideally, then, you should study your children, notice their tendencies, and offer opportunities to grow in those directions.

Then cheer them on and expect the best. But one more word of caution: make sure your expectations are realistic.

There's a fine line between expecting the best and the impossible. Scripture challenges us not to lose heart, and that's exactly what happens when we overchallenge our children. Though we should coax them to succeed, we must first ask, *at what?*

Are we sure they have the ability to accomplish what we're asking? Are we pushing them because someone else's children can already do what ours can't? Are we competing with others through our children or making decisions based on what we wish we'd done as kids? Or, worst of all, are we expecting perfection?

Why shouldn't we lower the bar for our children, since we regularly do so for ourselves? We can't expect a child to do what even we can't. One obvious example is controlling our emotions. None of us are experts at that, so we can't expect our children—who have much less experience and practice—to be good at it.

I (Margaret) remember that Lars, as a toddler, never liked his hair being washed. He didn't mind the sudsing-up part, but the rinsing upset him. Though I always lifted his chin and promised not to get water in his face, he would erupt in tears just anticipating that possibility. It all started because he'd had a water-swamping incident as a little guy and had panicked, feeling like he couldn't breathe.

My expectation was that he'd get used to having his hair rinsed without incident and would eventually stop objecting. But this was asking him to do something he wasn't yet able to do, not till he was much older and logic outweighed instinct. We struggled through those toddler bath times, when instead I should have pulled the plug on his daily hair washing.

Though Lars shared his bath time each evening with Nelson, who was two years older and didn't mind water over his head, I could easily have let Lars opt out most nights. No harm would have come to him had I washed his hair only once or twice a week, and he would have enjoyed bath times without so much anxiety.

Though moms ought not to expect too much, the opposite is true also—expecting too little. Children often live down to (or up to) whatever expectations we set, which is why it's critical to examine each situation accurately. This means having varied expectations for different ages, sexes, natural bents, personalities, temperaments, and skill sets. A wise mother will know who's who in her family.

The uniqueness of children is one reason they fascinate us. Some are malleable, like peanut butter. Others are unbending, like peanut brittle. Such radical differences definitely make your job more difficult, and you long for even one way you can treat your children the same without doing damage to somebody. Is there such a thing? The answer is yes.

One thing all children need equally is a mommy who's glad to be with them. During the early years, they can never get enough of you, and seeking your attention is their way of asking, "Do you still love me?"

They want to know, "Do you love me when I'm acting out? When I'm dirty? When I'm loud? Sick? Disobedient? Messy? Tired?" They're also interested in the flip side: "Do you still love me when *you're* tired? When *you're* sick? When *you're* working hard?" And they hope for a yes every time.

Raising children presents never-ending challenges, but as you do this important work, always remember: peanut butter and peanut brittle both taste good.

I pray that your love will overflow more and more,
and that you will keep on growing in knowledge and understanding.
For I want you to understand what really matters.
Philippians 1:9–10 NLT

What can you do today?

Write down one unique characteristic of each of your children, and tuck the paper into the pages of your Bible.

We wish we'd known . . .

1. sensitive children can be wounded in ways that will last a lifetime.
2. how a mother's words can either build up or destroy.
3. to eliminate all if-onlys.

Chapter 7

BEAT THE CLOCK

Teach us to number our days,
that we may gain a heart of wisdom.
Psalm 90:12

I (Margaret) will never forget the day my jam-packed schedule could have caused a fatality. Nelson (seven) and Lars (five) were at school, and I couldn't wait to get going on a long list of errands with Linnea (three). My efficiency had already been eroded by a workman's untimely arrival, someone we'd expected for weeks who had finally come to tile the bathroom.

After getting him started, I rushed little Linnea into the car, and she quickly scrambled over two rows of seats to the back section where children's books and toys awaited. (In the 1970s, car seats were not yet the law.) I started the engine but suddenly remembered my shopping list on the kitchen counter.

"Mommy will be right back," I said, glancing in the rearview mirror where Linnea was absorbed in a book. I bolted for the house and hadn't been inside thirty seconds when I heard a crash much like a fender-bender. Intent on getting my list, I didn't give it a second thought.

Several seconds later I heard a second crash and wondered if an accident was in progress on the street in front of our house. As I headed for the door, list in hand, the tile man shouted from the upstairs bathroom, "Hey! Your little girl is driving your car back and forth in the driveway!"

My heart stopped. Rushing into the yard, I saw our powerful Jeep Cherokee pressed hard against a small tree, which was now bending under the weight. My next-door neighbor was on the ground in front of it, frantically crawling backward from the base of the tree where she'd been planting flowers.

Though I didn't see Linnea inside the Jeep, I heard her crying. Flinging open the driver's door, I found her crumpled on the front seat holding her head. My mind was spinning with confusion, but I gathered her into my arms and reached in to turn off the engine.

Apparently, she had climbed back over the seats to the steering wheel and pulled herself to a standing position on the gearshift handle, notching it into Reverse. This Jeep had a fast idle, and it must have moved backward into the yard where it hit a sturdy oak. That probably knocked Linnea off balance enough to grab onto the shift lever again, pulling it one more notch down into Drive, which made the car move forward where it hit the smaller tree in our neighbor's yard. The goose egg rising on Linnea's forehead was evidence she'd fallen against the steering wheel as the car hit. I felt awful.

And it all happened because I'd had too much to do and was in too big a hurry—an injured child, a traumatized neighbor, an upset tile man, a damaged car, and a weeping mother.

No Time like the Present

Back in the 1950s, there was a black-and-white TV program called *Beat the Clock*. Adult couples raced against time while doing goofy stunts, like wearing a helmet with a ball on a string, then having to swing the ball into a bowl atop the helmet. A loud, obnoxious buzzer blared when their thirty seconds ran out.

As the mother of young children, you might feel much like those game-show participants, rushing through every day at high speed, trying to beat the clock. It doesn't help that your children are pros at putting obstacles in your path. Their frequent interruptions and many messes destroy your efficiency and discourage you to the point of losing heart.

What's a mommy to do?

Every so often it's important to take a fresh look at how you're running your home. What's most important to you? Are you tending to that particular thing amid everything else you have on your docket? How can you meet the demands of running a home and family without taking too much time away from them?

A good place to start is your calendar. What fits nicely into the sections of your day when you write it down but causes you to run like a hamster in a wheel when you're trying to accomplish it? Think of a bingo card with the center square marked *free*. Your schedule ought to be liberally dotted with free spaces, since you'll always need time to come up for air. Interruptions, emergencies, and accidents will dot your days, though you can't plan ahead for them. Intentionally putting spaces into your schedule is one way to proactively reduce the speed of your life.

Be ruthless about analyzing your calendar. You might even ask a friend to comb through it with you. What absolutely must stay? What can be whited out? What can be done less often? It's easy to mark time, waste time, or kill time. But can you buy time? We think you can, by eliminating what's unnecessary.

Years ago a friend (Margaret's) gave me a gift that showed how I could buy time. It was a coffee mug that said, *No, I can't bring 4 dozen cookies. Next question?*

Though I laughed at such a brazen statement, the underlying message was a good one. I needed to learn how to say no, even at the risk of offending someone who might not understand. Overcrowding my life and the lives of my children just to please another person was lopsided thinking. And when I took an honest look, I realized that many of my over-the-top commitments were simply because I enjoyed the praise of others. "How do you do it all?" sounded really good to me. I had to admit that I'd been prideful, which was painful to do. But it was the impetus I needed to begin again.

With years of practice since then, I've learned that saying no to one thing lets me say yes to another, even if it's yes to solitude. Try to determine what you want your yes commitments to be, and write them down. That will help you say no when you should, which is one surefire way to buy time.

REDEEMING THE TIME

How do we get the most out of every day without the frenzy of trying to beat the clock? The Bible speaks to this in practical terms. Psalm 39:4 says, "Lord, remind me how brief my time on earth will be. Remind me that my days are numbered—how fleeting my life is." God wants us to be cautious and prudent, living with an awareness of time ticking away.

He's telling young moms, "Make a careful analysis of everything to which you commit. The clock never stops, and you don't want to spend precious minutes pursuing things that aren't worthwhile."

You might say, "Most of my time is already earmarked for the things I absolutely must do, both at home and away from home. Making choices isn't part of it."

But there *are* choices. You can determine which time-soakers are optional and X them off your calendar, at least for now. And if you're wondering what litmus test to use in determining what goes and what stays, start by holding onto the commitments you share with your little ones during these early years. That might mean continuing to work on a church nursery committee where children are welcome at the meetings or signing them up for a preschool program where you are one of the helpers. It might mean volunteering in your community in a way that would benefit from the presence of your little ones.

I (Mary) used to volunteer for the local Meals on Wheels organization, packing and taking healthy meals to shut-ins. Though I'd wanted to do this from the time my children were little, I decided it would be too much to bring them along. Instead I waited till they were all in school. I could deliver the meals quicker that way and move on to the many other things I wanted to do.

Then one day, after collecting the packaged meals I was to deliver and shoving the overloaded bin into my car, I watched as another mom joined our crew of delivery ladies. She'd brought her two- and-four-year-olds along and was moving at their much slower pace. She handed one meal at a time to her little ones. "Carry this to Mommy's car now. Be careful, because there's a hungry lady waiting for us to bring it to her."

The example of this woman patiently letting her children help with this worthwhile project impacted me, and I stopped to watch. It occurred to me I'd missed a golden opportunity to teach my children some great lessons by waiting to volunteer till they were all in school. Meals on Wheels would have been the perfect way to teach an important character trait: helping those who couldn't help in return. And since most of the meal recipients were elderly, they would have been blessed to see the children. But I'd chosen to put efficiency above values, forfeiting that opportunity.

When you and your young children do things together, God counts this as "redeemed time." Including the youngsters He's given you elevates the activity to a level of His special blessing since you are joining with Him in acknowledging their importance. Children are little for only a short time, and those first five years fly by. So work to be deliberate about beating the clock, making that time count.

We aren't implying you have to be tied to your children every minute. It's essential (and healthy) for every mom to spend time with other moms, swapping ideas and building friendships. That often means sharing burdens during hard times and praying for one another. And since most young mothers occasionally experience feelings of isolation or loneliness at home with little ones, getting together with other women remedies this.

Adult conversation becomes especially meaningful after steady exposure to toddler babble or nonstop questions from a four-year-old. When you're confronted with a mothering problem, hearing a friend share how she dealt with the same thing in her child is a practical help, as well as a dose of encouragement. All moms need to know they're not the only ones struggling with child-rearing dilemmas.

Both of us remember participating in a once-a-month event for mothers and little children called "Coffee in the Park." It started with a handful of our church girlfriends plus their kids, each of whom were babies, toddlers, or preschoolers. After choosing a park with a playground suitable for small fry, the only instructions were, "Bring lunch for you and your children, and we'll see you there midmorning."

The crowd quickly mushroomed because these coffee breaks met several important needs:

1. Moms could share with other moms.
2. Children could play with other children.
3. Children could be with their favorite person—Mom.
4. No one needed to hire a babysitter.
5. Everyone could have a great time with very little effort.
6. And as a bonus, moms could know they were redeeming the time.

Of course there are those days when every mom needs a break from the stress of mothering—date night with a husband, a shopping trip alone, dinner with girlfriends. Don't feel guilty about taking time for these adult events once in a while. If you're meeting with people who need encouragement you can provide, you are redeeming the time in that way, too, while receiving nourishment yourself.

WHAT YOUR CALENDAR CAN SAY ABOUT YOU

- I'm too busy.
- I don't have any free time.
- I'm disorganized.
- I'm too rigid.
- I never do anything for me.
- I'm too self-centered.
- The children are too programmed.
- The children need to get into activities.
- I'm away from home too much.
- I never get out.
- I'm storing earthly treasure.
- I'm storing heavenly treasure.
- I'm neglecting my husband.
- I'm neglecting my kids.
- My kids are my whole world.
- I need to reach out to others.
- I'm living a balanced life.
- I'm completely out of balance.

We all get the same twenty-four hours each day, and it's up to us how we spend them. Scripture tells us to make good use of our time, and part of that is injecting joy into our lives. A wonderful verse for mothers is Proverbs 17:22 (NASB), "A joyful heart is good medicine." It's medicine that will keep you energized and motivated to be a great mom. And as you partner with the Lord to orchestrate the events of each day, He'll make sure to pour joy into your heart.

No Good Time to Worship Children

Babies, toddlers, and preschoolers are the most darling people on the planet. When your first newborn was placed in your arms, you probably studied her face with a sense of awe you'd never felt before. Taking in the wonder of a brand-new life is an experience words can't define. The scent, the softness, the helplessness, they're all intoxicating. As a mother holds a baby against her chest, she's lulled into a dreamlike world of wonder like no other.

And the amazement over children doesn't end when they leave their newborn days. Crawlers, toddlers, and those learning baby talk easily capture a mother's heart with their antics. Watching them is pure entertainment, and cameras click nonstop over every new achievement.

Then there is the charm of preschoolers with their endless (and often thoughtful) questions, many of a spiritual nature. Parents delight in watching them try to make sense of their narrow worlds and enjoy new abilities to do more things well.

Regardless of how infatuated a mom can be with her first baby, a second one often comes along just as she has thoroughly bonded with the first. She wonders how she can possibly love a second child as much as the first. But God's beautiful surprise is that love grows according to the need for it, and she ends up with more than enough for both.

But what is that first child's point of view when the second comes along? Just when she's getting comfortable at the epicenter of her adoring mother, along comes a sibling, and everything shifts. Visitors to the house brush past her to see the newborn. Pretty packages arrive, but they aren't for her. Cameras still click, but they're aimed in a new direction. And worst of all, when she tries to get close to her mommy, somebody else is always in the way.

When a New Baby Arrives

- Share your attention.
- Try not to favor the youngest.
- Find time for the older.
- Remember, each child is important.
- Let the older child help mom.
- Remind visitors to acknowledge the older child too.
- Avoid planting seeds of jealousy.
- Pray for increased patience.

I (Mary) can get completely infatuated with a newborn. To be honest, new babies touch me in a way no other age does. With the arrival of each one into our family, it was difficult for me not to get completely swept up in the needs of my infant. But one day, when our sixth baby had been snugly established on her newborn pedestal, God brought me up short.

Johanna, four at the time, watched me show off little Stina to one visitor after another. She heard my phone conversations about the blessing of the new baby and quietly observed how important she was to me. Then one day, as we were together at the grocery store and other mothers were oohing and aahing over little Stina, Jo quietly made a comment that changed my whole perspective. "I guess you don't want me as a kid anymore."

Not believing I'd heard her correctly, I said, "What did you say?"

She repeated her comment, and suddenly I realized how blatant I'd been in my lavish love for the new baby, to the point of hurting another little person I loved very much too. I felt terrible and learned my lesson that day. Though I still feel euphoric over newborns, I've worked to be more discreet when other children are in the room.

The clock is always ticking, and we know little ones don't stay little for long. It isn't difficult to idolize them during their cutest years, but never should we allow ourselves to worship them. It's a temptation faced by every mom who loves being a mom.

TIME DOES RUN OUT

I (Margaret) will never forget meeting an unusual woman at the grocery store years ago. Both of us had one-year-olds in our carts and found ourselves stopped in the same aisle. Her little girl and mine eyed each other cautiously, and we moms enjoyed watching them. I'd been shopping for a while, and my cart was mounded with groceries for our family of nine. This mom had nothing in hers.

"Wow," she said. "Look at all that food!"

"I'm almost done," I said. "And you must be just starting."

"Oh, I'm not here to shop," she said. "I just like to get out of the house. Motherhood is boring, and if I stay home, I just watch TV all day."

I was stunned. There sat her toddler, as eager to share time with her mommy as any other little child, and I wondered what *she* was doing when her mother was absorbed in TV all day. Letting this important time slide by without intentionally engaging with her child was a costly loss for both of them.

As you try to make the best use of the time you have with your children, especially during their first few years, it's important to remind yourself that time does run out. The day will come when your children no longer live with you, and your role as their mother will have shrunk significantly. Though they hang on your every word now, during the teen years they may not be interested in your opinion at all. You have a powerful influence when they're little and can use it for good, or you can waste it. In later years you'll wish you could get it back.

Moving through your busy days, carefully consider the brevity of this stage in your children's lives. If you get discouraged or feel overwhelmed, remind yourself there will come a day when you'll have all kinds of free time to use any way you please. We've both reached that point, and even with lots of children, in-law children, and grandchildren, each of us can arrange for big chunks of quiet alone time without too much trouble. Your day will come too. Meanwhile, pour your energy into raising your children well.

Now Is the Time for God

I (Mary) love to study God's Word, and I especially love to do it with other women. I've been attending well-organized Bible studies for forty years, always bringing my preschoolers along. But there were periods of time when I should have backed away from those weekly meetings, times when commitments at home should have taken precedence.

I remember a day when I was once again headed for my weekly Bible study class with two little ones in the car. I'd worked hard that morning to get Julia (four) and Karl (two) ready for our early departure, but an overnight blizzard was slowing us considerably. Driving to the church just a few miles away proved to be a major challenge, but we pushed forward anyway. As always, I was eager to spend the morning studying the Bible with other women. The kids loved their Bible programs too.

When we pulled up to the church, we were already quite late, and it irked me I couldn't find a parking spot. Because of deep snowdrifts everywhere, many of the usual places weren't available. Cars were parked every which way, and though I threaded my way around the church several times, our morning of Bible study wasn't to be. With frustration building in both the children and me, I decided to just head home. It dawned on me then that maybe home was the best place for us to be . . . at least on that day.

Group Bible studies are wonderful, and I still attend them. But young mothers often stretch themselves too thin by trying to get up and out to too many activities. Like us, you've probably been schooled to stick with your commitments and step around any obstacles in the way. But the flip side of that is like swerving around danger signs that say "Road closed ahead," then hoping against hope you don't go over a cliff.

God looks at your heart. Do you sincerely want to know Him better? Do you want to glean wisdom from His Word? Do you want to hear what His will is for you? If so, He will gratify your longings. He's pleased when you choose Him over other commitments and will make a way for you to get to Him when it seems impossible. He'll also guide you in setting godly priorities with your time and in your family.

When I (Margaret) had all seven children at home, I continually failed to have private devotional time with God. I tried meeting with Him after all the kids were in bed at night, but that only resulted in me falling asleep too. I tried the early-morning thing, but it never failed that one of the children would wake earlier than usual and need me.

I tried naptimes, but babies don't coordinate their sleeping habits with toddlers, and getting them all unconscious at the same time didn't happen often. Besides, if I used naptime for my devotions, when was I to catch up on all that had been left undone during the morning? Still, I knew I needed God's steady stream of advice if I wanted to be a good mother.

Meeting less and less with the Lord, I began playing out the dilemma in my mind. The Lord loved children, sending each one as a special gift. But He also wanted to meet with me. I worried about keeping Him waiting while I continually tried to get to Him without success.

Then one day my heart heard from God. *I can meet with you smack dab in the middle of your crowded days.*

He filled my mind with biblical examples. "Didn't I meet with Peter out in a boat? And didn't I counsel my disciples at the beach? Don't you remember how I chatted with Zacchaeus in a tree and taught two men on a long walk? I've had meaningful meetings with people in gardens, on mountainsides, during dinners, in courtrooms, on roadsides, and in cemeteries. Can't you and I talk like that?"

I felt as if I'd had a devotional aha moment, and my heart surged with hope for success at learning from the Lord. Maybe He would talk with me as I peeled carrots or calm my spirit while I folded laundry. Maybe He'd instruct me as the kids and I raked leaves or shoveled snow. And if I was watching for Him, He might minister to me in the middle of the night as I fed a baby or rocked a feverish child.

Eager to go along with God's idea about meeting me throughout the day, I tucked a Bible into the bathroom drawer and read verses as I fixed my hair. If I was interrupted, I knew the Lord understood and wanted me to deal with the disruption but then continue with Him. I also knew He wouldn't be offended if I stopped to tie a shoe or doctor a skinned knee. I put another Bible in the car, where I could glance at it while waiting for a freight train to pass or an older child to come out of school.

I dusted off an old radio from the basement and set it on the kitchen counter, tuning it to a Christian station. God met me on the airwaves, not just through sermons, interviews, and two-minute devotionals, but through inspiring music too. Even pushing my double stroller around the neighborhood was an opportunity to sing my favorite hymns or hum worship choruses, often with children joining in. Weeding flower beds was a chance to thank God for the wonders of His world and tell Him how much I appreciated the things He'd made.

The more ideas God put in my head, the more I saw that His creativity was far greater than mine. And my relationship with Him started to come alive. He began solving many of my problems and dispersing nuggets of wisdom just when I needed them. He delivered inner peace amid chaotic circumstances and heartfelt joy in simple, everyday experiences.

How to Find Time for God

- Restrict time on social media.
- Watch for small pockets of peace to connect with God.
- Ditch the idea of a perfect quiet time.
- Know that God doesn't hold it against you if you can't meet with Him.
- Believe that quick "arrow prayers" have power.
- Worship through hymns and choruses.
- Tune in to Christian radio.
- Keep trying.

God knows when you really want to get to Him. Proverbs 8:17 says that anyone who looks for Him will definitely find Him. And in that same verse He says something sweet to urge you to try. "I love those who love me."

In other words, when you seek Him out, He views that as your way of saying, "I love you, Lord, and I really need time with you, but I just don't have anything extra." In response, He'll love you back by somehow making time available to you. An overcrowded calendar or glitches in your schedule don't limit His ability to get to you in any way. Just ask, and He'll surprise you by bringing the two of you together.

Psalm 145 says, "The Lord . . . is filled with kindness . . . close to all who call on him, yes, to all who call on Him in truth . . . He hears their cries for help and rescues them" (vv.17–19 NLT). He's standing by, waiting for you to call on Him in a cry for help. But the key to success is within *you*. Do you really want to connect with Him or are you comfortable keeping your distance? Are you letting things other than your children distract you from God and His Word? Like TV shows? Phone conversations? Social media?

Test yourself. See if you can keep the TV off and set your phone in a drawer for an hour or two. Can you do it? If you can, include electronic fasts like that as part of every day. And if you can't, ask yourself two questions: What's so important that I absolutely must look at it? And why?

God offers to pour blessings into your life and into your mothering efforts if you'll only seek Him sincerely. Allowing other things to push those supernatural gifts away is a loss you will one day regret. Both of us have experienced delightful surprises from the Lord that nourished us when we felt depleted by motherhood's demands. He has lavished confidence on us after failures and let us know what to do in sticky situations. There's nothing He can't do and no difficulty you can't manage when you ask Him to steer you through it.

So put a Bible in your bathroom drawer and prepare to be amazed. God will connect with you in all kinds of new ways, and He won't insist that you beat the clock in order to meet with Him.

There is a time for everything,
and a season for every activity under the heavens.

Ecclesiastes 3:1

What can you do today?

Revive yourself with a piece of chocolate.

We wish we'd known . . .

1. to do less alone and more with children.

2. to put strict limits on outside commitments.

3. to view interruptions as opportunities.

4. that personal pursuits could come when children were older.

Chapter 8

SPOON OUT THE SUGAR

Pleasant words are a honeycomb,
sweet to the soul and healing to the bones.
Proverbs 16:24 NASB

Before I (Margaret) had children, I never knew toilet training could be fun.   Birgitta, our seventh, was nearly three when she pleaded with me to wear big-girl panties. It took less than a week for her to figure it out, and I was proud of her, rewarding her with M&Ms.

Toward the end of the week she came running from the bathroom, all excited. "Mama! Come and see what I made!"

Though I was thinking what you're thinking, when I got there it was something else.

"Look!" she said, pointing to the toilet water. "Blue and yellow made green!"

Sure enough, our blue toilet cleaner had combined with her yellow pee-pee to turn the water green. I started laughing, delighted to share in her joy.

Children are full of fun and frequently try to pull us into it. Joining them doesn't cost a thing, and there's no learning curve. All we have to do is get on board with the good time they're already having.

Make Your Home a Happy Place

We want happy homes, and we hope our children will one day look back and say, "I had a great childhood." What can you do now, while they're little, to get that end result? Not that hilarious fun has to be the order of every day, but what can make your home a haven for a family who's happy to be there?

One thing we've found helpful is looking for the humor in whatever happens. Even the messiest situation usually has a giggle buried in it, which goes for the endless mini crises that come a mom's way too. Of course, if someone falls from the top bunk and breaks a wrist, that's not funny. But most of what frustrates young moms isn't as exasperating as it seems.

When we look back in our old photo albums, we're reminded of both failures and successes. One thing we see clearly, though, is that children are inconvenient, especially when they're little.

Each day seems to drain away your full supply of energy and determination. Even so, it's good to recognize now that these demanding days will one day be gone, and you'll look back with longing.

When I (Mary) was a new mom with only one child, Luke wanted to be my right-hand man in everything I did—just like all two-year-olds. My goal that day was to make a batch of pepparkakor cookies, a traditional Swedish favorite. The dough must be rolled thin before using cookie cutters to make shapes. I planned to involve Luke by giving him his own ball of dough and hoped he'd be content with that while I got the cookies made.

What I hadn't counted on was that his attraction to the flour was greater than to the dough. As I dusted the cookie cutters, he dusted his hands, face, hair, clothes, and everything within a ten-foot radius. My kitchen was quickly deteriorating, but I decided to let him do what he wanted and gave him his own scoop of flour.

He poured and spread and patted his treasure until it had puffed itself wall-to-wall. But I got all my cookies baked, and Luke had thoroughly enjoyed himself. Cleanup was significant, but that particular photo in my album tells of a success. Luke's big smile, shining through his floured face, says, "Mama and I had fun today!"

Dealing with a wide variety of messes in the wake of our children's good times isn't the end of the world. Usually the kids can participate in cleaning up too, which can become a secondary kind of fun. Accept that they'll slow you down, but recognize that a slower pace is the best way to share time with the very young. If you want to be a fun mom, you have to accept that it'll take extra time. Our suggestion is to let kids be kids, and snap a picture *before* cleanup. Even if it isn't funny then, it will tell a colorful story later. Besides, when your children are grown and insist they never gave you a lick of trouble, you'll have proof.

Another suggestion for a happy home is to include music. I (Margaret) used to calm fussy babies by swaying and singing to the radio at our dance parties for two. And since even nonfussy children love to swing and sway, my dance card was always full. Appropriate music did something special for me as a mom, too, soothing frazzled nerves and bringing a certain sweetness into the room.

Use lively music during tidy-up times to make kids move faster, and challenge them to get the toys put away before the end of a song. They all love a race.

Sing lullabies or Sunday school choruses with (or to) your little ones at bedtime. Both of us used music tapes (cassettes back then) to coax preschoolers into sleep after we'd left their bedrooms. Some of them learned Scripture during these last moments of the day by hearing short verses sung to simple melodies.

We mothers have the lofty privilege of setting the tone in our homes. Music can factor in nicely when we choose to hum or sing as we work. It lifts us above the drudgery of housecleaning or doing dishes ... again ... and promotes a cheery atmosphere around us, which is where the children usually are. Little ones are keenly perceptive to the moods of adults and are especially influenced, positively or negatively, by how mommy is feeling. So whistle while you work and bring a bit of extra pleasure into your home.

Fun Things to Do with Kids

Age 1: rock, sing, look at picture books, put objects in and out of containers, play pat-a-cake, peek-a-boo, this little piggy, horsie

Age 2: lie in the grass to watch the clouds, visit a construction site, go to a zoo, pour water, color bath water, read books

Age 3: take walks, visit a pet store, play dress-up, visit a children's museum, shape clay, string beads, attend library story hour

Age 4: draw with sidewalk chalk, go for a picnic, create a treasure hunt, paint a driveway with water, spray snow with colored water, invite friends over

Age 5: get a library card, bake cookies together, organize toys, color, paint, make mud pies, plant seeds, build a fort, create a pretend store

One more idea for promoting happiness is to guard your tone of voice. Joyful enthusiasm goes a long way toward promoting upbeat moods. Your voice can be soothing, demanding, lilting, playful, or harsh, which is why speaking the same words can send different messages. So lean toward cheerfulness as you talk to your kids.

And as you make a conscious effort to have a happy home, remember to smile at your children. It sounds like a given, but watch yourself as you move through a day of mothering. Note how often you smile at them, eye to eye. Grins from mommy nourish their young spirits and often cause them to smile back. That, in turn, nourishes *your* spirit, and you've become part of a cycle of happiness.

Scripture says that the person who makes an effort to refresh someone else—whether by voice, smile, kind words, or selfless deeds—will be refreshed themselves (Proverbs 11:25). So work hard to make your home a happy place, and you'll find yourself happier too.

MAKE YOUR WORDS POSITIVE

Everything you say to your children has the power to either build up or tear down. Once harsh words have been spoken, the damage is done, and no amount of positive words can undo it. Though a child might take it in without any outward show of emotion, inside, one of two things is happening. Either she is suffering deep pain or feeling intense anger, and her mother may never know.

A young child idolizes her mother and wants to please this person she loves more than anyone else in the world. Childhood wounds that come from damaging words can put someone on a psychiatrist's couch years later. Children crave the nourishment of positive words, especially from their mothers.

I (Margaret) remember how good it felt when one of my kids said thank you or I love you. Best of all were words of willing cooperation. When Birgitta was two, she adopted the lovely habit of saying "OK" to virtually every one of my requests. If I said, "Birgitta, would you come here, please?" she'd immediately respond, "OK, Mommy," and come. Or, "It's time to clean up your coloring now," and she'd say, "OK, Mommy," and do it. I began calling her my OK-girl, and that seemed to please her.

As I remember it, she was the only one of my seven children who always complied without resistance. Tossing out a directive to several of the others was cause for bracing against a catalog of excuses detailing why they couldn't comply, at least not then.

But Birgitta was my OK-girl.

That's why it was easy to speak positive words back to her. "Honey, every time you say 'OK, Mommy,' it makes me happy, and I know it also pleases Jesus. Thank you for your cooperation. I really appreciate you!"

But what about those who respond negatively? They need good words too. So what do you do if the situation calls for constructive criticism? You've accepted the challenge to train your children and want to take advantage of every opportunity. When they need a parental adjustment, rather than yelling at them or saying things you might regret later, think of the old song, "A Spoonful of Sugar": "Just a spoonful of sugar helps the medicine go down."

That's not a bad philosophy when it comes to correcting children. Though you may disapprove of what they've done or refused to do, mix praise with your criticism. Make sure they know you still love them by sweetening your statements with approval. "Usually you're such a good helper, so I know you won't throw that doll again." Deliver the goods, but always do it with a little sugar.

The Bible says, "Gentle words are a tree of life" (Proverbs 15:4 NLT). The opposite is also true. "The words of the reckless pierce like swords" (Proverbs 12:18 NIV). If you want to nourish the souls and emotions of your children and avoid needless anger, determine you're going to choose gentle words over harsh ones, and the atmosphere in your home will be sweet indeed.

MAKE YOURSELF SAY YES

Once you've tuned in to saturating your family with positive words, you'll want to carefully consider the grand champion of all positives: the word yes.

Most children long to have a yes-mom, but most moms don't want to be one. Saying yes translates to extra time, extra cleanup, and extra patience. But moms should remind themselves that the yes word brings a few positives, too—extra fun, extra laughs, and extra joy on the faces of the children.

Of course a mother can't always say yes. "Can I have a cupcake right before dinner?" or "Is it OK if I ride my trike alone to the store?" But sometimes saying yes is easy. "Can we color my bath water? Can I get the Play-Doh out?"

Take care not to become a mom who specializes in no, denying requests just because you can. And if you're not up to a yes at that particular moment, say no, but put a positive spin on it. "Yes, we can get the Play-Doh out, right after your nap."

If you give out lots of yeses, your children will gradually get the sense that you're in their corner and want to say yes whenever you can. That, in turn, makes them more understanding when you have to say no. Children are drawn to fun people and gain a double blessing if their mom is one of them. So take full advantage of the yes word, an easy way to bring a lighthearted spirit into your home.

Make Fun Memories

What's the key to making happy memories with your children? One easy win is to say, "Would you like Mommy to play with you?" Any young child will light up hearing that. Even better, though, is if Mommy herself comes up with a playful idea and springs it on them when they least expect it. "Hey, sweetie, would you like Mommy to teach you how to play hopscotch?" Or "Shall we rake up a giant pile of leaves and jump in it?"

Kids respond with delight to creativity in their moms, and the wilder the idea, the more they love it. If it involves getting dirty or making a mess, that's even better.

I (Mary) remember one December when our family was packed up to make a trip two states away to visit my husband's side of the family. The five kids we had at the time were pumped for the trip, but at the last minute, inclement weather forced us to cancel. We were disappointed, so I racked my brain for something that might lift everybody's spirits. The children and I ended up driving to a place called The Plaster Hang-up, where shoppers could buy unpainted plaster figures and paint them. For a small fee you could sit at long tables full of paints and brushes, after which the staff would spray each creation with a protective coating.

Because it was Christmastime, we decided on a group project: a nativity scene. Each of us picked a plaster-white character from the shelves and did our best that afternoon to paint Mary, Joseph, and company. The result was a unique nativity set no one else in the world could match—not that anyone would want the rainbow-colored cow or cockeyed wise man. But we had a fun afternoon and made a memory that's still fresh decades later, because that nativity is on display every December.

Of course no family can manage nonstop hilarity or constant yeses. Every mom has work to do, and sometimes she has to say no. She usually can, however, set up play situations nearby while she's doing something else. Both of us have dressed our toddlers in big garbage bags, stood them on chairs in front of the kitchen sink, and let them play with water, bubbles, and measuring cups while we got other things done close by. A quick glance at what they were doing, accompanied by a few words of affirmation, satisfied them. "Honey, you poured that water really well. And did you see rainbows in the bubbles? Didn't God make them pretty?"

BENEFITS OF HAVING FUN WITH CHILDREN

- Builds strong relationships
- Keeps mom young
- Presents opportunities to teach
- Provides release of stress
- Brings shared laughter
- Builds happy memories

Another way to make happy memories is to promote the holidays. Enlist the children to help decorate the house. Encourage them to wear red, white, and blue on Memorial Day, green on St. Patrick's Day, and lavender on Easter. Let them squeeze the food coloring into pink scrambled eggs on Valentine's Day, and set a penny by each dinner plate on Lincoln's birthday. Hunt for any excuse to have a good time with your kids.

But here's one sensible word of caution: beware of December! If there were such a thing as motherhood do-overs, both of us would go into that first Christmas as mothers with greater care. We absolutely overdid it, and it didn't stop with just celebrating the day. Eventually the entire month of December grew into one giant wave that took us under. To be brutally honest, we both grew to dread the Christmas season. What a terrible thing to say! But it was exactly what we deserved for trying to outdo ourselves every year. We wanted our kids to have fun, but fifteen gifts apiece is more fun than any child should have.

Eventually we agreed to start over and settled on three gifts for each child from three categories: practical, spiritual, and fun. With presents coming to them from other sources too, nobody suffered. Less became more, and the frenzied ripping open of gifts no longer happened. Another benefit was that the spiritual gifts gave us more of what we'd wanted all along: a Christmas focused on Jesus, not on our children.

Don't let December's month-long celebration run you ragged with its endless possibilities. Even standing in the checkout line at the store can be risky with all the holiday magazines tempting you: 101 CHRISTMAS CRAFTS or HOMEMADE GIFTS MADE EASY.

Not that we're against homemade gifts, especially for teachers and relatives. They have definite advantages—not just at Christmas but anytime—especially if the recipient loves children. But choose your projects wisely and make them precious few.

When might it be wise to undertake handcrafted gifts with your youngsters? And why?

The why is easy. It's one more way to spend valuable time with your kids and offers another opportunity to praise their work. Making simple gifts also keeps you and your brood out of stores with long checkout lines, frustrated shoppers, and high prices. Besides, homemade items have a way of hanging around for years, reminding both you and your children of the good time you had making them.

Homemade is always more personal, too. But just like with the plaster nativity set, keep your expectations realistic and let the children do their thing, regardless of the result. Grandma and Grandpa will love it no matter what it looks like. After going over the top as we did, our advice is to choose just one easy Christmas project each year and let the rest of those alluring magazine ideas go.

Homemade Beats Store-Bought

- Personalized books
- Decorations
- Outfits reflecting holidays or nationalities
- Party planning
- Birthday cakes
- Gifts for others
- Any food made with your child
- Children's artwork, matted, framed, and autographed

One way to happily involve children in the holidays without ever touching your scissors or glue is to let them help prepare for guests. It's a surefire way to build enthusiasm for the event, even if they aren't familiar with the people coming. Ditch perfection and let them help you set the table, choose the napkins, and arrange seasonal decorations.

Don't worry if the end result looks like something off the pages of Dr. Seuss. Your children will be more excited than if you'd hired a professional party planner, and your guests will find it all charming. Best of all, you will have spent meaningful time with your kids—a treasure beyond measure.

Christmas isn't the only holiday that can get out of hand before you realize it. Birthdays, too, can grow exponentially. I (Margaret) remember excitement building as our firstborn was about to turn one. Since I wanted our whole circle of friends to share in this important milestone, moderation went out the window. Mary's second child, Julia, was born that same month, so we decided to have a blow-out, double-whammy party.

We invited a dozen children with their families. That meant about forty guests, since most couples had more than one child. We cooked two dinners, one for the children (in the playroom) and one for the adults (in the dining room).

The night before the party I stayed up past 4:00 a.m. baking and decorating a school bus cake that my son would never remember. Mary arrived with a spectacular doll-shaped cake for little Julia, having done the same. Though we had fun decorating the tables, planning games for both children and adults, and preparing the meals, by the end of the party we were ready to drop. It never occurred to me that this first-birthday extravaganza was setting a dangerous precedent.

> ## IDEAS FOR SUCCESSFUL BIRTHDAY PARTIES
>
> - Begin small.
> - Invite same number of guests as child's age.
> - Hold party when birthday child is rested.
> - Serve a kid-friendly menu.
> - Play age-appropriate games.
> - Plan parties less than two hours long.
> - Gear everything to children, not adults.
> - Enlist a friend's help.

Consider the end before you begin. To make happy memories, you don't have to go hog wild. A wise guideline for a party guest list, for example, is to invite as many friends as candles on the cake. In other words, Nelson and Julia should have had one baby-guest apiece. What a calm, less exhausting celebration that would have been.

MAKE THE GOOD TIMES ROLL!

I (Mary) encouraged my children to play outside and get to know nature on an everyday basis. Though they might stray a ways from the house, we lived in a friendly neighborhood with a group of moms who looked out for each other's kids. Even my toddlers were "free range" and enjoyed animals and plants in a variety of ways.

One day little Karl (eleven months) was crawling around the yard, staying close to cousins and grandparents who were there too. Every so often he'd stop to finger a bug or poke the ground with a stick, but never did he fuss or cry.

The next day I was changing his diaper and got the surprise of my life. Lying there was what looked like a white wire, and I wondered how he could possibly have swallowed it without injury. But when I bumped it with the corner of the diaper, it moved! My shriek caused my husband to come running, and he quickly identified it: a night crawler. Karl had eaten a garden worm.

Giving children the freedom to explore does carry risks, but usually they're minimal. Karl never suffered from his unusual meal, and we continued to let him crawl around the yard with minor supervision.

A small child operates in his own world of wonder. He hasn't had time to learn much, so he's on a continual quest to add to his experience. That prompts him to use his favorite skills: touching and tasting. He's on a mission to get to the bottom of things, and as he tries, he learns. Putting restrictions on his natural curiosity is to stunt his growth, at least in terms of how he thinks about his world.

Not long ago we posed a question to our fourteen adult children, one that could have had fourteen different answers. Though they used a variety of words, they all gave essentially the same reply. We asked, "What was the best thing about your childhood?"

A few of the answers: "You let us run free. You didn't hover over us all the time. You let us explore. You encouraged us to play outside. You let us roam the neighborhood. You let us run wild."

This surprised both of us, since we'd expected them to mention other things, like specific holiday traditions, favorite family vacations, even baking cookies with mom. But there it was. What meant the most was being allowed to do what all kids yearn to do: satisfy their curiosity.

As always, we caution you to use common sense. If you live near a busy street, it's logical your children will need firm boundaries. If you have a swimming pool, they should know how to swim. If you live in the country, they need to know how far they can stray.

But as often as you can, let them learn by investigating life by themselves. And when they come running, out of breath with excitement over something they've discovered, stop what you're doing and share their wonder, even if it's only for thirty seconds. As you listen to them, it'll make you smile, and it's very possible you'll be handed an opportunity to turn their attention to the Creator.

"Mommy! Mommy! I found some gold! Some *real* gold!"

"My goodness! Can I see? Wow, that does look like gold. Let's pretend it is. Isn't it shiny? Did you know that God uses real gold to make the streets of heaven? What do you think those will look like?"

It's moments like these, stockpiled over years of time, that build a child's understanding of the awe-inspiring person in charge of nature. And God Himself frequently initiates these moments by way of a child's discoveries.

Often we parents think the best way to make children happy is to plan something for them: a party, a play date, some screen time. There's nothing wrong with those, but first choice ought to be just giving them time to play. It's a good idea for kids to learn to entertain themselves, too, figuring out what to do with unscheduled time. As they practice this, they'll come up with all kinds of creative ideas, some that will astound you.

I (Margaret) loved the creativity in Louisa when she thought of making food art. It started while she was sitting at the kitchen table letting me know she had "nothing to do" while I fixed dinner. Fingering a bowl of fruit on the table as she talked, she absent-mindedly arranged and rearranged it, first by color, then by size, then by type. Eventually she asked if she could put the fruit on a large tray to make it pretty.

It wasn't long before she was nosing in the fridge for grapes and blueberries too, and little by little an entire village took shape on the tray. She used veggies and any other bits of food she could find, including rolled deli meat. In the end we took pictures but then put everything back where it came from (slightly worse for wear), and she'd enjoyed exercising her creativity. As for me, I was given the perfect chance to praise her for a project well done. I could also point out that God loves variety.

Children love any excuse to celebrate life, whether it's arranging fruit or making mud pies. I (Mary) always kept a baker's squeeze-bag of frosting in the refrigerator. If we made a cake, it took only seconds to write something on it—*Happy Spring!* or *Hooray, no cavities!* We also wrote names on cookies or made happy faces on banana bread. But their favorite was frosting squeezed on their fingers or palms, a simple way to make an ordinary day special.

Most moms spend a great deal of time in their kitchens, which brings her young children there as well. This is the one room in the house that has unlimited potential for interesting experiences, some of them extremely important:

- It's hot! Watch out!
- It's breakable! Be careful!
- It's cold! Close the fridge!
- It's sharp! Don't cut yourself!

These cautions become valuable lessons learned when mommy is available to rescue if necessary. On the plus side, her kitchen often smells good and can even be the source of interesting sounds. The endless array of tools she uses is fascinating to children, and there's always the chance she'll ask for help. One easy way to give children a good time is to let them join you in meal prep. Teach them how to use a dull knife correctly, giving them soft foods to practice on (a banana or muffin). Let them stick toothpicks in tiny cubes of cheese or stir the brownie mix.

THE CHILD-FRIENDLY KITCHEN

- Small table and chairs
- Child-size apron
- Plastic dinnerware
- Small, sturdy stool
- Toy bin
- Paper and crayons
- First-aid kit
- Low-hung chalkboard

Put some thought into equipping your kitchen for pint-sized partners whose greatest joy is to be where you are. Whenever it's reasonable, let them take part in the action. As you show them how, gradually they'll learn the right way to do things, but more importantly, they'll bond tightly with a mama who knows how to make the good times roll.

The cheerful heart has a continual feast.
Proverbs 15:15

What can you do today?

Surprise your children by having ice cream creations for dinner. (If you feel guilty about all the sugar, sprinkle fruit on top.)

We wish we'd known . . .

1. that saying yes doesn't spoil kids.
2. that small children are happy with mom's attention and need little else.
3. how easily a mother's words can wound her child.

Chapter 9

BALANCE THE SCALES

Let your moderation be known unto all men.
The Lord is at hand.
Philippians 4:5 KJV

I (Margaret) remember the day I'd made a platter full of
PB&J sandwiches for our Saturday lunch when my first three
children were ages four, six, and eight. A handful of neighbor
kids were also at the table, and a lively debate was in progress.

"My dad is stronger than yours," said one.

"No he's not," said another. "My dad can lift me and my
brother at the same time. That's stronger!"

"Yeah, but my dad is *older* than yours," another said. "He's fifty!"

"That doesn't matter," our four-year-old Linnea said, "because my dad weighs 200 pounds!"

Case closed.

Bigger is always better with children. And if you ask them "How much is enough?" they'll all agree, "A lot more."

LET MODERATION WORK FOR YOU

If there's one thing children don't have and badly need, it's balance. Truth be told, adults often have the same problem. If some is good, more must be better. But the Bible describes a different standard.

In 1 Corinthians 6:12 it says, "I have the right to do anything . . . but not everything is beneficial." So even when it's not wrong to have more, bigger, or better, it's not always good for us. It can lead to extremes with harsh consequences, which is why mothers are charged with teaching their children to live in the middle ground of moderation.

For example, as fun as it is to buy gifts for your children, you ought never to give them before they're ready. A two-year-old who doesn't know his numbers shouldn't be given a watch. A three-year-old who doesn't understand a camera shouldn't own one. Pushing gifts ahead of a longing for them eliminates much of the joy they will feel when given something they've wanted for a long time.

Moderation and self-control are closely related, since the first requires the second. In teaching this principle, Scripture offers a picture of the immoderate person by comparing him to a dog. A dog is always willing to eat another helping of food, and another and another. He knows nothing of moderation and will eat himself sick if given the chance. God's Word equates this excessive behavior to wickedness in a passage that describes evil people acting like dogs. "The dogs have a mighty appetite; they never have enough . . . they have all turned to their own way, each to his own gain" (Isaiah 56:11 ESV).

So how do you go about teaching your children to be moderate when their natural leanings are toward excess? First, make sure they don't become the center of your home and family. That spot is reserved for Jesus Christ. Certainly each person is an important part of the whole, but no individual ought to be regularly exalted above the others.

Once you've established that the world doesn't revolve around your kids, focus on modeling character traits that will lead them toward moderate lives: patience, humility, and contentment. For instance, if you hope to teach contentment but find yourself complaining in front of your children, more than likely they'll follow your example. If you voice dissatisfaction over your home, your car, your clothes, or anything else, don't expect them to be satisfied with what they have.

Children are pros at playing "Follow the Leader" and will gradually reflect your behavior. Living a moderate life is difficult, and sadly, the extremes are much easier. For instance, instead of carefully controlling your voice volume when admonishing children, it's easier to shout. As difficult as it is to land somewhere in the middle, that's the route to a life without regrets.

Working toward moderation—both in yourself and your kids—even has a few perks. Use it as a tool to balance your family's schedule, for example, as you decide how much time you want to spend away from home chasing after classes, sports, lessons, or other activities. A moderate plan might be to let each child have one outside commitment each week, but only one.

If they have a single focus, they'll be able to put greater effort toward the activity and avoid being spread so thin they can't do anything well. That way you avoid the trap of living in your car and also the endless shopping for all the supplies they need—two definite perks. It's also nicer to your bank account.

But what if you're the kind of mom who wants her kids to have more activities than just one at a time? What if you like lots of action? There's nothing wrong with that, though it pulls your attention away from home. But it can be dangerous if your children aren't like you in that regard.

Attempting to push them beyond their interests or capabilities causes unnecessary stress, both in you and in them, and they're going to object. Don't push them to unhealthy limits in the name of doing what you think is good for them. Leading little ones to overcommitment outside your home can have far-reaching, negative consequences. It's a much better idea to promote moderation.

SIGNS OF OVERLOAD IN PRESCHOOLERS

- Tearfulness
- Nervous tics
- Disinterest in play
- Withdrawal from mom
- Excessive clinginess
- Insomnia
- Reverting to infant behavior
- Tantrums
- Unrealistic fears

Moms can also push their kids too hard in areas other than organized activities. They might force socialization before a child is ready or demand instant obedience without a moment's grace. Parents can urge academic learning beyond a youngster's ability or push a child to move faster than he's able. And if a mommy gives a directive using words a little person can't understand, confusion and frustration result.

If you decide to operate in the middle ground, moderation will work for you, bringing blessing to your children, your family, and yourself.

LET MOMMY SET THE PACE

When Marta and Stina were ages three and five, I (Mary) decided they owned far too many stuffed animals. I thought it would be a good exercise to give some away to less fortunate children, a process that would also clean out a closet that resembled a zoo, with fifty-plus animals in residence.

I sat the girls down and outlined the plan, not sure how they would respond, but both liked the idea. Starting with a mountain of big and small animals, we dove into the project with enthusiasm, lining them all up on their bedroom floor. "Each of you choose the ones you'd like to give away," I said, "and I'll pack them up."

I watched as they handled each kitty, doggie, and bunny, obviously struggling to let go of what was rightfully theirs. Eventually they brought me a couple of the rattiest-looking animals in the bunch, the ones that were closer to trash than donations. I felt a strong urge to criticize their poor choices and felt like saying, "I can't believe you picked the worst-looking animals you have! Both of you are selfish, and I'm disappointed in you." But I sensed God nudging me to take the opposite approach.

"That's great, girls. I know it's hard to give away what belongs to you, but it's the right thing to do, since you have more than you need. Some children have none . . . but now they will!"

Praising them did several good things. It let them know I understood how hard it was to give away their toys. It also built them up inside, which was evidenced by their big smiles at my positive response. And it was just the motivation they needed to go back and choose a few more animals to give.

Mothers have the priceless privilege of setting the mood in their homes. We've all heard the truism, "If mama ain't happy, nobody's happy." That's because God blessed women with the ability to read people well. If the mood is low, she knows how to lift it. If it's tense, she knows what will soothe. If it's high-spirited, she knows how to keep it under control.

Along with this valuable skill, however, she has the responsibility to use her power wisely. If children already feel bad about something, she can choose to make things worse or better. It might make her feel better to make them feel worse for a moment, but that would be an abuse of power.

Remember that negativity feeds on itself and starts a downward spiral that's hard to stop. Your children will pick up on it and think it's impossible to please you. When they feel they can never do anything right, they'll give up trying and will feed their own negativity right back to you.

So what should you do? Identify your stress points and work to eliminate them, or at least reduce them. Ask your husband or a good friend for how-to suggestions. Their objective analyses might lead you to solutions you wouldn't have thought of yourself.

AGE-APPROPRIATE CHORES

Age 1
- *They* are a chore.

Age 2
- Putting bits of trash into waste can
- Family "gofer" (go and get)
- Putting toys away
- Picking up sticks in the yard
- Getting the mail

Age 3
- Entertaining younger sibling
- Picking up, putting away
- Unloading dishwasher with mom
- Making own bed
- Bringing dirty clothes to the washer

Age 4
- Carrying in the groceries
- Vacuuming
- Sweeping
- Feeding pets
- Putting their clothes away

Age 5
- Setting the table
- Putting groceries away
- Dusting
- Clearing the table
- Emptying waste baskets
- Helping with a younger sibling

Some days you'll feel like you're wrapped in a heavy blanket of stress much like the lead shield a dentist lays on you before an X-ray. It isn't easy trying to divide your limited time between husband, children, friends, church, job, housework, and other things you'd like to do. But if you ask God for help, He'll show you where to find balance.

He might send others to assist you, so take advantage of whatever is offered. Would that high school girl down the street come play games with your kids for an hour after school? How about that lady at church who enjoys your children so much—might she be willing to come one afternoon to read to them? What about Grandma and Grandpa? If they live a reasonable distance from your house, might they be willing to take on a weekly gig at their place, allowing you time to be home alone? Or would your husband agree to "man the fort" early in the morning before going to work while you take a walk around the neighborhood?

Ways to Reduce Stress in Mommy

- Get up ahead of your children.
- Ask your husband to help in one specific way.
- Pencil in some mommy time.
- Resist feelings of guilt for time alone.
- Nap with your little ones.
- Talk with another mother.
- Hum a tune.
- Sneak a piece of chocolate.
- Enjoy a hearty laugh.
- Listen to worship music.
- Go to bed earlier.

Though you want to be careful not to overcommit outside your home, the opposite is also true: you don't want to isolate yourself by never going anywhere. One gift the Lord has given all mothers is a desire to spend time with other women. If they have children of similar ages, the connection is even better. Friends in the same life-stage can encourage you, problem-solve with you, and empathize with you. You can do the same for them.

A simple way to spend time with friends without hiring a babysitter is to meet in a child-friendly park, moms and kids together. We scheduled this kind of thing regularly with friends, and each time we gathered, our time together was valuable. Since some of us had older children with school schedules and carpools bookending our days, these gatherings were just a couple of hours, but they did us all a world of good.

How else might you inject bits of joy into your life as a mom? Both of us have given ourselves mood lifts by such simple things as lighting a candle with a pleasing scent or setting a small vase of wildflowers on the kitchen counter. Throw pillows with words of Scripture on them fed our souls. A cut-glass heart or faceted sphere hung in a window flashed rainbows across a room when the sun hit it, a stunning reminder of God's close presence.

During cold weather we sometimes made a small fire in the fireplace. The smell was a tonic and its crackle like cheerful music. If the house was a mess, we'd set the kitchen timer for three minutes and work with the children to tidy one room, putting everything away. Clutter can cause greater stress than a dirty house.

Both of us kept a favorite greeting card in a drawer for when a laugh was needed. Mine (Mary's) was a musical one with *I Love Lucy* and Ethel on the front. When I opened it, these two pals would break into song: "Friendship! Friendship! Just a natural blendship . . ." Each time I needed a lift, I'd open it once again just to get a little burst of warmth and joy.

My card (Margaret's) showed two women standing at a bus stop, one a rocker-type with multiple piercings, work boots, spiked hair, dark glasses, and skimpy clothes. Next to her was an old grandma clutching a purse and wearing a babushka on her head. The rocker looks at the oldster and says, "Good morning!" The grandma says, "Don't hurt me!" I still have the card, and it still makes me laugh.

Take full advantage of the freedom you have to establish the atmosphere in your family. As you use this power in positive ways, home will become their favorite place to be.

LET LITTLE ONES BE LITTLE

I (Margaret) was completely enamored with our firstborn, Nelson. By the time he'd grown into a pudgy six-month-old, I had to force myself not to idolize him. I wanted to watch him every minute and thought his moves were cuter and smarter than any other baby on the planet.

One day I decided it was time for him to begin crawling. Several of my friends' babies had crawled by six months, and I didn't want him to fall behind his peers, so I began conducting short training sessions here and there throughout each day. I'd put him on all fours and then try to move his knees on the carpet in a crawling pattern before he went flat. Over and over I worked with him while he giggled with pleasure at this focused attention from his mommy.

After several weeks (and rug burns on all four of our knees), I gave up in disappointment, wondering if he might be one of those babies who skipped crawling and went right to his feet. But a couple of weeks later, after inching himself along on elbows and tummy for a while, he surprised me by learning to crawl on his own.

As a first-time mother, it had never occurred to me that Nelson would eventually figure out how to crawl and walk all by himself, and that tutoring wasn't necessary. As soon as he became physically ready, a desire was born within him and he began trying. Shortly after that, it got done.

My problem was wanting to push little Nelson through his babyhood faster than he could go, rather than just enjoying each phase as he was in it. Many moms feel the same. They can't wait for the next bit of independence and end up not appreciating their baby's here-and-now. Don't throw away today by longing for tomorrow.

Help for You

- Neighbors
- Well-chosen screen time
- Grandparents
- Personal Exercise
- Daddy's helping hands
- High school helpers

Every mother hopes to raise her child to be a fully functioning, independent adult, and the most effective way to accomplish that is to refuse to push them toward the next goal. The best route to independence is to first satisfy a child's every dependent need.

I (Margaret) once watched a hurried mother brisk-walk across a big parking lot, her toddler in tow. The little guy's legs were a blur as he tried to keep up with the big strides of his mommy, but he was failing. She seemed unaware of his struggle, and every few feet she gave him a yank and a *hurry up*, as if he was dawdling or resisting on purpose.

This little boy was doing his best, but it wasn't long before she was tugging him so hard that his feet literally left the pavement. This insensitive mother needed to acknowledge that her child wasn't ready to do what she was asking. And the solution would have been easy. She could have carried him, pushed him in a cart, or slowed her pace.

Little children need to be allowed to be little. Even Paul of the Bible spoke about this. He wrote, "When I was a child, I spoke and thought and reasoned as a child. But when I grew up, I put away childish things" (1 Corinthians 13:11 NLT). In other words, acting your age—even when it's only one or two years old—is the way it's supposed to be. When the time is right, life will insist that childish things be put away.

I (Mary) was determined to get our firstborn, Luke, toilet trained before his second birthday, because a new baby was on the way. I had three months to get him out of diapers and into pants before my due date, and I set to work with enthusiasm.

I arranged a play station for Luke in front of the toilet: a plastic TV tray with different activities like modeling clay, picture books, and small cars. In the beginning I found all kinds of things to do in the bathroom while Luke sat on the toilet and played, but gradually my confinement got old. Both of us were prisoners because I'd bought into peer pressure that said children should be toilet trained by two.

After many weeks, Luke finally did get the hang of it. But looking back, my fear of having two kids in diapers was ridiculous, and it would have been easier on both of us had I waited another six months or even a full year.

BABY FEELS GOOD WHEN

- She's with mommy.
- His tummy is full.
- He's rested.
- She's warm.
- He has something to look at.
- She's sucking.

Resist putting pressure on your child for any reason. It becomes a problem for him and also for you, and it promotes the lie that every child should grow through his stages on a schedule. Scripture says, "There is a time for everything . . . [God] has made everything beautiful in its time" (Eccl. 3:1, 11 NLT). If you want to succeed, wait for the right time and refuse to rush things. When your child is ready, both physically and emotionally, success will come quickly.

There's a unique wonder to every phase of a little one's life, and it's best if we can find gladness and contentment in each one. If we push too hard, the result will be unnecessary stress in both mother and child. And it can go beyond that, surfacing in a child through nervous habits, irrational fears, or withdrawal from Mom.

LET CHILDREN WORK

The world of children spins far slower than that of adults, and in their opinion, slower is always better. Rushing spoils everything. I (Mary) remember whining to my husband about all the work I had to do when our children were young, and he said, "Why don't you enlist the workforce you have right here at home?" Growing up on a farm, he'd worked hard alongside every other member of his family, and he assumed his own children would pitch in too.

I was reluctant, knowing they wouldn't work up to my standards, but I went ahead and made chore charts anyway. Then we began spending Saturdays checking off the jobs. Marta was four when I assigned her to do some of the vacuuming. As a toddler she had loved a little game we played where she ran from the vacuum and I chased her with it. She'd been pleading to use the vacuum ever since, so that was the perfect chore for her.

Of course, turning sophisticated equipment over to children does include risks. Marta frequently ran over the vacuum cord, which allowed the beater-bar to chew it up in several places. In due time, the cord—duct-taped in four spots—had to be replaced, but it was worth it to see Marta eagerly learn to vacuum well . . . and eventually she learned to go under, not over, the cord.

We can almost hear you groaning as we suggest putting your young children to work. Talk about a slowdown! Pint-sized helpers can be a real drag on your schedule. But it's best to pull them in while they have the want-to, and young children have plenty of that. Though they can make your work twice as hard and productivity half as good, it's still a practical idea to include them. Why? Because once you put them to work, those everyday chores get elevated to something more than just mundane maintenance.

When *Not* to Push It

- Is it beyond his ability?
- Does she understand what your words are saying?
- Is he exhausted?
- Are you exhausted?
- Are you reacting rather than acting?
- Is she getting sick?
- Can the battle be won?
- Are you in a rush?

Working with your children gives you the opportunity to build them up with praise, which deeply nourishes them. They want to be with you more than with anyone else, and working on a project together is more important to them than a group activity or lesson of any kind, especially during the early years.

Your children will gladly take all the time you're willing to give. Though you'll sacrifice efficiency when they help you, you'll be pleasing the Lord as well as them in two ways. You'll be training them as He instructs mothers to do and showing love in yet another way.

THE BENEFITS OF CHORES

- Experience joy in helping.
- Feel like part of the family team.
- Learn about serving, not just being served.
- Enjoy being a genuine help to mom.
- Acquire valuable skills.
- Practice finishing what was started.
- Find satisfaction in looking at a finished project.
- Bask in mom's praise for work well done.

But there's more.

Believe it or not, young children can be a real help to you. As you let them work, they'll get better and better at what you ask them to do. And they'll love learning big-people jobs. All of a sudden, it'll dawn on you that they really are a genuine help. Children who do household chores also enjoy being part of the family team, pulling some of the group's weight, and they'll take pride in the orderly home they help create.

Children who do chores will also get to experience the deep satisfaction of accomplishing something by working hard. Insisting that they help diminishes the entitlement mentality our culture so boldly promotes as you acquaint them with the rewards of purposeful work.

Just be careful you don't take this idea too far. Children have no power to resist a parent who's making unreasonable work demands, so be sure their assignments are moderate and well matched to their ages. Balance responsibility with ability and try to inject an element of fun along the way.

For example, if you assign a child to clean the bathroom faucets and drains, tell her you're going to check her work by using the faucet chrome as a mirror to put on your lipstick, and invite her to watch you. Or when he's done sweeping up dust bunnies, encourage him to put socks on and slide across the wood floors. Or maybe after she's helped to unload the dishwasher, you'll let her choose one of those clean bowls and enjoy a scoop of ice cream.

When You Pray

- God hears your prayers.
- God cares about ordinary things.
- God sees everything at all times.
- God usually requires you to wait for answers.
- God does answer your prayers.

Think of your children as young apprentices watching you and listening to your instructions. In the process, they'll begin appreciating everything you do for them in new ways, which is one of the unexpected perks of letting them help. And if you work alongside them, you can demonstrate perseverance and problem-solving as you go, two skills they'll take all the way into adulthood.

Be sure to have child-appropriate equipment on hand for their use—a short broom and miniature dustpan, small spray bottles, nontoxic cleaning products, stools of different sizes, and child-size aprons. As they work, they'll learn it's not that easy to do what you do. Though they'll love squirting the Windex bottle, it'll take some practice to clean every smudge off the glass and get the corners well. And they'll find out there are many stages to getting laundry from the hamper to the washer, through the dryer, and back into dresser drawers.

Speaking of laundry, I (Mary) used kid power to lend a hand with dirty clothes. Since the hamper was on the main floor and the washer/dryer in the basement, I put my kids in charge of tossing dirty laundry down the steps. A couple of them were so young I worried they'd fly down along with the clothes, but thankfully that never happened.

Shouldering a bit of responsibility on wash day gave them a sense of helping the family and taught them that work can be fun. As for me, I no longer had to carry a heavy hamper down the stairs.

I (Margaret) never minded doing the wash but was endlessly frustrated over trying to get the clean clothes back into multiple rooms and drawers. Finally I decided the children should do it.

I said, "I'll continue to wash your clothes, but from now on you'll have to take them back to your rooms." We had two preschoolers at the time, along with three grade-schoolers, and gradually (with me assisting the little ones), all the loaded laundry baskets made it to their rooms. What I hadn't anticipated was that they simply lived out of their baskets, rifling through the clean, folded clothes without putting anything away.

When Children Work

- Demonstrate exactly how to do each job.
- Make expectations clear.
- Let them make their own mistakes.
- Never redo their work.
- Allow your house to look lived in.
- Lavish praise over every success.
- Keep criticism to a minimum.
- Let perfectionism go.
- Work alongside them.
- Reward finished work.

So one day I decided to fall back on my tried-and-true method for getting results: bribery. I called them all to the kitchen where a laundry basket of clean, folded clothes awaited each one. "Put these things neatly into your drawers." I said. "If you bring your empty basket back in three minutes, you can have a candy bar. But I'll be inspecting your work afterward, and if you've stuffed your drawers, no candy." (Of course there was grace on the neatness score for the young ones.)

While the kids watched, I slowly lined up miniature candy bars on the kitchen counter, then said, "One . . . two . . . three . . . GO!"

The littlest needed help carrying, but most grabbed their baskets and stumbled over each other in a mad rush to meet the deadline. My candy-bar system worked like a charm for many years and eliminated an irritating chore for me.

So enlist your children as junior helpers. Though the end product of their work won't rival yours, little by little you'll have some mighty fine helpers. And just knowing they're contributing something to the family will diminish your sense that mommy does all the giving and children do all the taking. That, in turn, will help you balance your mothering scales and lessen your stress.

Follow God's example, therefore, as dearly loved children,
and walk in the way of love.
Ephesians 5:1–2

What can you do today?
Step outside and take five cleansing breaths.

We wish we'd known . . .
1. to develop a strong work ethic earlier.
2. that our work as mothers would spill over into future generations.
3. not to hurry our children through the stages of childhood.

Chapter 10

BUT JESUS WAS
NEVER A MOTHER

The LORD always keeps his promises; he is gracious in all he does.
The LORD helps the fallen and lifts those bent beneath their loads.
Psalm 145:13–14 NLT

There's never a good time to have the flu, but it's especially bad when the sick person is a mom with young children. My (Margaret's) first three kids were ages one, three, and five when the stomach flu found me kneeling in front of a toilet for the third time that morning. Nelson, our oldest, was having his own struggle, wrestling with an unruly sock in an effort to get dressed for the day. I sensed his mood deteriorating, but my own "project" required my full attention.

A few seconds later, midvomit, I caught a glimpse of him stomping toward me. "Mama?" he said in a demanding voice. I couldn't answer, so he said it louder. "Mama!"

Snatching a quick look in his direction, I saw he was holding up a striped shirt and plaid pants—it was the 1970s.

"Does *this* go with *this?*"

Still I couldn't answer as I hung over the toilet.

"Mama! Does this *go?* Does it *go!*"

My only thought was that motherhood had sunk to a new low.

When this kind of bottoming out occurs, most moms think, "I never dreamed it could be this bad. Doesn't anyone understand what I'm going through?"

The answer is yes, but you might be surprised at who. It's Jesus. And we don't mean because He's all-knowing and all-seeing. Believe it or not, He experienced all the struggles you have. That doesn't seem possible, since He was never a mother, but if we carefully follow Him through the pages of Scripture, we see it.

JESUS IS LIKE A MOTHER

Jesus lived with His twelve disciples around the clock. He trained them for the future and worked with them as they practiced what He taught them—exactly what you do with your young children. And He had twelve of them!

In John 13:33, He addressed this group as *my children*, and indeed they were. Acting quite childlike, they made demands of Him, questioned His decisions, were selfish, robbed Him of His privacy, resisted His teaching, became argumentative, were stubborn, and pestered the daylights out of Him. Sound familiar? They also disobeyed Him, were the cause of intense frustration, and at times were a disappointment.

Like you, Jesus provided food for His "children," comforted them, guided their decisions, wept over them, prayed for them, and loved them passionately. Despite His perfect parenting, they often got the best of Him. (Even perfect parenting doesn't guarantee perfect children.)

As we listen to Jesus speak to His disciples, we hear Him mothering them much like you mother your children:

1. *Don't you remember?* (Matthew 16:9 NLT)
2. *Why are you arguing with each other?* (Matthew 16:8 NLT)
3. *Don't you know or understand even yet? Are your hearts too hard to take it in?* (Mark 8:17 NLT)
4. *You are seeing things merely from a human point of view, not from God's.* (Mark 8:33 NLT)
5. *You have eyes—can't you see? You have ears—can't you hear? Don't you remember anything at all?* (Mark 8:18 NLT)
6. *You faithless people! How long must I be with you? How long must I put up with you?* (Mark 9:19 NLT)

7. *Why do you keep calling me "Lord, Lord!" when you don't do what I say?* (Luke 6:46 NLT)

8. *Have I been with you so long, and you still do not know me?* (John 14:9 ESV)

9. *Don't you understand? Why can't you understand?* (Matthew 16:9, 11 NLT)

Since Jesus spent all day every day with His disciples, He craved occasional time alone. Does that ring a bell? He sacrificed sleep or walked long distances to get away for a spell, sometimes hiking on rocky terrain up a mountainside (in sandals). Inevitably, though, when He finally did get alone, His "children" found him. Here's a sampling:

1. *Jesus slipped away into the hills by himself.* (John 6:15 NLT)

2. *When they found him, they said, "Everyone is looking for you."* (Mark 1:37 NLT)

3. *He left in a boat to a remote area to be alone.* (Matthew 14:13 NLT)

4. *Early the next morning Jesus went out to an isolated place . . . and when they finally found him, they begged him not to leave them.* (Luke 4:42 NLT)

5. *He went up into the hills by himself to pray. Night fell while he was there alone.* (Matthew 14:23 NLT)

6. *The crowds [disciples included] found out where he was going, and they followed him.* (Luke 9:11 NLT)

The ever-present mob was often too much for Him. Even at the end of a long day serving others, Jesus was so closely surrounded by people that He couldn't take a step in any direction:

1. *As Jesus was on his way, the crowds almost crushed him.* (Luke 8:42 ESV)

2. *A large crowd followed and pressed around him.* (Mark 5:24 ESV)

3. *After they had come down the mountain, a large crowd met Jesus.* (Luke 9:37 NLT)

4. *A huge crowd of people [was] coming to look for him.* (John 6:5 NLT)

5. *They had been waiting for him.* (Luke 8:40 NLT)

6. *So many people [were] coming and going that Jesus . . . didn't even have time to eat.* (Mark 6:31 NLT)

7. *The crowd got into boats . . . seeking Jesus.* (John 6:24 ESV)

You may feel the same way, that you're continually pursued by a crowd of persistent little people. Even if you do manage to get a minute to yourself, you know they're searching for you and won't quit till they find you. And when they do, even that might not be enough. Often, they want your body . . . your lap, your arms, your hip, or just your legs to cling to.

Scripture tells us that crowds of people were continually begging Jesus to let them touch Him, hoping He would fix their problems, which sounds much like a mommy's assignment.

Can't you just see Jesus, hands coming at Him from every direction, reaching for any part of Him from shoulders to feet? *Jesus! Just a quick touch!*

Matthew writes, "They begged him to let the sick touch at least the fringe of his robe" (14:36). Crowds begging, reaching, touching, pulling. He definitely experienced what you're going through today.

How well I (Margaret) remember the feel of a preschooler's finger poking into my sleeping body in the middle of the night. "Mama?" I'd hear, in a whisper. (Poke, poke, poke.) "Mama? I had a bad dream. I promise not to wake you up, but can I sleep in your bed?"

Sometimes that child-sized finger felt like a red-hot poker. Jesus understood. On at least one occasion He said, "Someone touched me . . . Power has gone out of me" (Luke 8:46 ESV). After a day of being tapped, tugged, and touched, you too might feel like the power has gone out of you. Jesus can relate.

And what about the endless questions you have to field every day? "Mommy, can I have . . . buy . . . do . . . go . . . take . . . bring?"

Jesus experienced the same. Everywhere He went, people were after Him for something. *Jesus, can you heal my child? Jesus, can you mend my relationship? Jesus, can you come home with me? Jesus, can I come along with you? Jesus, can you save me? Jesus, look over here! Jesus, turn around! Jesus!*

A young mother we know heard her mommy name so many times in one day that she asked her child to use her first name for a while. She thought if she heard one more mommy request, she'd go over the edge. Jesus gets that, which is why He hopes you'll ask Him for stamina, patience, advice, inner peace, or anything else you need. He's been there and done all that.

Jesus Wants You to Love and Trust Him

In Isaiah we read, "The Lord still waits for you to come to him so he can show you his love and compassion" (30:18). These are two excellent reasons to move toward Him: His love and compassion.

As you read the following definitions of those traits, remind yourself that this is how God feels about you. Love: *a profoundly tender, passionate affection for another person with a feeling of warm, personal attachment.* Compassion: *a feeling of deep sorrow for another who is stricken by misfortune, accompanied by a strong desire to alleviate the suffering.* (www.dictionary.com)

It might help you understand the Lord's connection to you by thinking about your love for your own children. Most likely you have a *profoundly tender, passionate affection for them with a warm, personal attachment.* And when they're suffering, you *have a strong desire to alleviate it.* Now magnify those feelings for your children by a thousand; that's what the Lord feels toward you. And let's not ignore one last comparison. Though most mothers love their children so much they'd give their lives for them, Jesus actually did so . . . because of His fervent love.

This one who loves you that much extends an invitation to you today. "Come to me" (Matthew 11:28). "Talk to me" (Philippians 4:6). "Trust in me" (Proverbs 3:5).

Experience God's love and compassion by taking Him at His word and looking for His influence in your days and nights. Believe it or not, the God of the universe wants to empower your mothering efforts, and it pleases Him greatly when you reach for Him in the small minutes of time you have.

How well I (Mary) recall our daughter Stina's consuming desire to be with me when she was a toddler. At times I felt like I'd grown another leg as I emptied the dishwasher or dug in the garden. Although something other than me could distract her for a minute or two, mostly she just wanted me.

I didn't appreciate being the object of such affection at the time, but looking back, I see it as pure, unconditional love. She trusted me 100 percent, never worrying about where her next meal would come from or if she'd be warm enough at night. She was confident I would anticipate and meet her every need.

In the morning, I loved lifting her out of her crib, feeling her warm body against mine, and enjoying her tender pats. I know God allows mothers to experience these feelings toward young children with the hope they'll understand the magnitude of His love for them.

Just as a baby wants to be close to and in touch with her mother, we can desire the same closeness to Him. Babies show us how to rest peacefully in arms with no trace of worry, which is exactly how we should rest in God's provisions for us—without a smidgen of worry.

But how can you get close to God and stay in touch with Him when you have precious little time to spare? The answer is to take advantage of minutes that pop up here and there. After pushing a pencil on this, we figured out that spending just five minutes in prayer each day and ten minutes in the Bible translates to ninety-one hours and fifteen minutes pursuing a relationship with God each year. Ninety-one hours!

TAKE THE LOAD OUT OF LAUNDRY

- Put a hamper/bin/basket/box in each bedroom.
- Mark a laundry basket with each person's name.
- Teach children to bring dirty laundry to the washer.
- Show them how to sort by color.
- Let kids pour detergent into the washer and push the buttons.
- Enlist children to put away their clean clothes.
- Keep bleach and other chemicals hidden.

I (Margaret) used to be burdened by one particular verse in the Bible. As a young mother with no free time, it hung over me like a daily threat, and I felt I could never do what God was asking. Luke 12:48 says, "When someone has been given much, much will be required in return." I knew I'd been given many blessings, so I also knew God required me to give much back. But I didn't know how I could with the minimal time I had.

The children He'd given me—who were indeed great blessings—subtracted the time I thought I needed to have a healthy devotional life with God. But the exciting insight He provided was that since I hadn't been "given much" in the way of extra time, God was not requiring much of my time in return. Understanding the verse in that flipped way released me from self-imposed pressure and evaporated the threat. Since I didn't have much time during those busy days, He promised to take what little I offered and turn it into something powerful.

> ### WHAT MAKES FOR GOOD DEVOTIONS?
>
> * A bit of time
> * An open Bible
> * A tender heart
> * A ready mind
> * A willing spirit
> * A reliance on God

All the Lord wants from you is a small amount of daily movement toward Him. In return, He'll share His wise counsel and meet your every need with fresh ideas and unexpected provisions. Complicated devotional times never work for young moms. But if you're eager to communicate with Him, He'll make a way. And as you take advantage of the bits of time you do have, remind yourself of the old adage that little becomes much when God is in it.

GOD WILL BRING SUCCESS TO YOUR MOTHERING

I (Mary) recall a simple bedtime prayer our four-year-old Stina prayed one night. It revealed her simple but full-on faith, the same kind of faith Jesus praised in Matthew 18:3 when He said, "Unless you change and become like little children, you will never enter the kingdom of heaven."

Stina had full confidence that everything we told her about Jesus and God was infallible truth, and her prayer that night was an example of that. Her grandpa had died recently, and we'd talked about him being in heaven, living with Jesus. So at the end of her regular bedtime prayer, Stina tacked on a special request. "Oh, and please say hi to Grandpa."

We chuckled at her words that night but were pleased to see that God had successfully helped her make the leap from our words to her own belief system. It was an example of how He brings success to parenting when we are faithful to teach them what the Bible says. Stina had come to own an important biblical principle: that there's life after death, and that for believers, it's a good life to be with Jesus.

No parent has a storehouse of flawless wisdom, though, and none of us can count on parenting success every time. But

God does have one of those storehouses, and thankfully, He's eager to share His riches of wisdom with us any time we ask.

The Lord is delighted that you want to be a good mother and hopes you'll partner with Him throughout the process. As you ask for advice, He'll give it to you. Psalm 32:8 says, "I will instruct you and teach you in the way you should go; I will counsel you with my eye upon you" (esv). He's got His eye on you and is offering to help you succeed.

Be patient as you watch for positive results. Think of how patient He is with you. Although He looks for spiritual growth in you based on what He's taught you, He's willing to wait as long as a lifetime without ever giving up on you. He's never in a rush, which is sometimes cause for frustration in us as we pray and hope to see certain changes in our children. But maybe the reason He's often slow to answer prayer is that we're slow to learn—children and adults alike.

Mothers need to be become experts at waiting. It's an opportunity to show the same patience God shows toward us. Spiritual fruit will come to your children if you keep calling out to God on their behalf without giving up or doubting. And His answers, whenever they come, are always worth the wait.

PRINCIPLES TO PASS ALONG

- Knowing and loving God trumps everything else.
- God's Word is life's trustworthy guide book.
- People are more important than things.
- Children are gifts from God.
- No one can out-give God.
- Count your blessings every day.
- Love without counting the cost.

God knows the exact weight of the load you carry. He knows where the line is that causes blessings to morph into burdens. Nothing surprises Him, and He is well prepared for every eventuality. The rub comes when a day is going badly, and you don't sense Him entering in. It's at those times you should remind yourself He's as close as your right hand. He has told us, "I am the Lord your God who takes hold of your right hand and says to you. Do not fear; I will help you" (Isaiah 41:13). All we need to do is look down at our hand and say, "You've told me you are *that* close, Lord, and I'm going to trust that's true."

If you bump into more failures than successes, take another look at your expectations. Maybe you're "hanging the hay too high for the goats," as the farmer said. In other words, your children may be trying but failing because they can't reach your high standards. Check with your parenting Partner, and He'll tell you exactly how high to hang the hay.

The Father Calls You to Motherhood

One of the charming (and sometimes humorous) things about young children is their complete honesty. Though this can be an embarrassment to adults, their tendency to say what's on their minds gives parents a peek into their hearts.

It's a sobering thought that everything you say and do comes to them as infallible truth. That's because you are their first image of God. As you answer their endless questions, be aware of the powerful impact your words are making.

I (Margaret) recall watching four-year-old Louisa furrow her brow over something that was bothering her. "What's the matter, honey?"

"If you die and go to heaven before I do, how will I know where to find you?"

It was a valid question and showed she'd been thinking about what we and others were teaching her. She had completely accepted that heaven was a real place where both she and I were going someday. She also knew we probably wouldn't go at the same time.

As I was contemplating a good answer, her face brightened and she said, "I know! When I get there, I'll look for Jesus. Then how 'bout if you be standing next to Him?"

She figured Jesus was in charge of heaven, and everyone there would know who and where He was. I quickly agreed to her plan, and she skipped off to play.

Scriptural Encouragement for You

- Jeremiah 29:11
- Proverbs 3:5–6
- Joshua 1:9
- Psalm 116:1–2
- Jeremiah 33:3
- Psalm 68:19
- Romans 8:38–39
- Philippians 4:19
- 2 Corinthians 9:8
- Psalm 145:18–19
- Romans 8:28
- Jeremiah 31:3
- John 15:26–27
- Hebrews 12:1–3

Preschool children are deeply spiritual. Ask God to guide you to good (and reassuring) answers to their questions, always sticking to the truth. Even more than that, though, try to live a consistent life in front of them. Your little ones are forming their opinion of our heavenly Father by scrutinizing everything you say and do. If they see godliness modeled in your example, it will be easy for them to transfer their trust in you to a trust in God.

God loves children. He could have increased the earth's population by somehow delivering full-grown people but chose instead to start us all as adorable mini humans. And despite the unending needs of babies and little ones, He hopes parents will take as much delight in them as He does.

Some mothers fall into motherhood by complete accident—or at least that's what they think. Actually, God is keenly involved in every conception and sovereignly orchestrates the arrival of every individual to the planet, and He doesn't stop there. Long before delivery day, He has good things in mind for each child and hopes that as they're being raised, each one will be taught how deep His love is for them. He puts families together in a variety of ways, but each is His thoughtful creation, including which position a child holds in the family lineup. None of it is accidental.

God set it all up the way it is and wants to bless your efforts to be a good mom. Because of His intentionality and involvement, your job of bringing up children is elevated to a high and honorable calling. His Word urges you to eagerly love them and cheerfully sacrifice for them, which is what He does for you—and them.

As you work to do it well, many of your sacrifices will go unnoticed, at least for now. No one may be watching or giving credit, except, that is, your children and your Lord. Kids recognize genuine love and thrive in its presence. And on those days when you feel put upon and underappreciated, know that God sees your work and keeps accurate books. He'll reward your diligence and will honor you for your faithfulness in making motherhood one of your highest priorities.

FEARS OF YOUNG CHILDREN

- Abandonment
- The dark
- Monsters under the bed
- Strangers
- Medical procedures
- Loud arguments
- Rough handling
- Thunder and lightning
- Physical pain

The effects of your mothering will go on indefinitely just as a pebble thrown into a lake produces ever-expanding ripples. What you do for a single child will have an influence on more than just that one. Because of that, mothering is ministering, which is one reason Jesus invites you to use Him as a model. He never gave up on His disciples but continued to train, serve, lead, and work with them, preparing them for the world they would influence after He was gone.

While He was with them, Jesus took every possible chance to interact with young children in front of the twelve, taking His time, letting them know—by His desire to be with little ones—that they were every bit as important as grownups. His body language showed that, too, as He took them in His arms. And His words were potent one-on-one blessings to them. After that, just in case His twelve "children" still didn't understand,

He made it clear that if anyone harmed a child in any way, they'd have to deal with *Him*.

God has put you in charge of His nursery. All children ultimately belong to their heavenly Father, but He's entrusted their care to earthly parents. A loftier calling than that there could never be.

EARTH OR HEAVEN, WHAT DOES YOUR HEART DESIRE?

I (Mary) loved attending Bible studies with my preschool children. First and foremost I was learning from God's Word, but secondly, my children were learning too. The well-managed children's programs taught Bible stories, choruses, and short verses.

How well I remember talking with Marta, our seventh child, when she was only two. The children's leader had told the morning's Bible story through the mouth of a little lamb puppet who was a familiar friend to the class. "I will be with you always," the lamb said, giving voice to their memory verse for that month (Matthew 28:20 NASB). Again and again the lamb said the line, coaxing the children to repeat it after her.

On the ride home, Marta and I discussed that morning's lesson—as much as a two-year-old with minimal vocabulary can. "What did you learn today, Marta?" I said.

In baby talk she said, "I will be with you always."

Not quite sure of what she said, I asked her to repeat it. How thrilling it was to hear Scripture come out of the mouth of our baby! Then I took it a step further. "*Who* will be with your always?"

She didn't hesitate. "The little lamb!"

One prayer Christian mothers pray is that their children will eventually receive salvation from God and walk daily with Him as Lord of their lives. In the beginning, children scramble much of what they're taught, but bit by bit, it makes sense. Years down the road, Marta would understand the truth of the puppet's biblical sentence, but not without being told who said it, under what circumstances, and to whom. And it would be later still before she would learn to apply it to her life.

Sow Scripture into Their Hearts

- Urge children to memorize verses.
- Create motions to go with each passage.
- Put Scripture words to simple melodies.
- Listen to Bible verses on CD.
- Keep verses short.
- Memorize a verse for each alphabet letter.
- Recite verses during daily tasks.
- Reward success.
- Memorize along with your children.
- Review, review, review.

Spiritual development comes at a snail's pace and usually includes setbacks. But the prayer for children to follow Christ as Lord will always be a good one. Actually it's the best prayer request we could ever bring to God's throne room. Meanwhile, what can be done to facilitate their walk toward Christ?

One important thing is to provide a Christian community around them. Take them to Sunday school and church. Read Bible stories at home. Chat about biblical principles as you go about your daily life. Listen carefully as they ask questions. Answer simply but honestly. In other words, do your best to put Jesus in their path, making it easy for the two of them to meet.

Conversely, be vigilant about what else they're exposed to that might be contrary to biblical values. Be cautious about what comes to them in the way of movies or other electronic entertainment and carefully screen their friends. If they join another family for a birthday party, ask about the agenda and who else will be there. Best-case scenario? Volunteer to attend the party too, as a helper.

If you use a day care center, don't assume a certain level of care without checking on your child often, especially before he's old enough to tell you what happens there. Make frequent unannounced visits and ask lots of questions. Whenever your children are not with you, it's critical to know who will be planting seeds in their young hearts and minds and what kind they will be.

The world criticizes a "mother-hover" like this, insisting she will create children who are fragile hothouse plants unable to withstand the cold, cruel world. But new seedlings *need* hothouses to protect them from too much too soon, and so do young children. Sheltering them during their most vulnerable years isn't overkill. It's wisdom.

Most of all, remember that much of what they learn in the early years is by watching and listening to you, so it's important to check yourself to see what you're passing on to them. Actions speak louder than words, and sometimes those actions speak so loud, your children can't hear a word you're saying.

How to Pray for Your Kids

- Pray for solutions.
- Pray the details.
- Pray daily.
- Pray over a sleeping child.
- Pray believing God will answer.
- Pray your child's name into Bible verses.
- Pray anywhere.
- Pray about everything.

Like it or not, every day you're telling them a story. As they observe, they have no trouble figuring out what's most important to you. They know who or what you live to please, and often they'll fall in line behind the example you set.

It's important to walk your talk. If you tell your children you dearly love Jesus but then never mention Him, your words teach hypocrisy. If you make household rules but break them yourself, they learn it's OK to buck authority. This nonstop observation might be nerve-racking, but it's actually a valuable part of the Lord's plan in sending children to families. He hopes you'll want to be a good example, and knowing that children are watching is a powerful motivator to live right.

The early years of your child's life are foundational to the rest of it. So take advantage of this tender time to build their trust in a loving God.

I (Mary) wish our family had had a mission statement while our children were growing up. I regret not sitting down together and coming up with one overarching sentence we could have used as the standard for everything else. Every decision could have been set next to that statement as a guide for the many choices we made.

Strong families often have a theme. It runs through the years like embroidery floss through a tapestry. Maybe it's "Family First" or "Others before Self" or "Take Personal Responsibility" or "Memorize God's Word." What do you want your family to look like? Certainly Christian families want a theme that's compatible with Scripture. Jesus said the two commands that really matter are to love God and love others. Decide together how you hope your family will do those things.

If I (Margaret) had the chance for a mothering do-over, I'd push for a mission statement like this: "Pray about Everything" or "Talk to God Daily" or "Nourish Life with Prayer." We could have set up a family prayer journal of requests and answers as the centerpiece of our home. It took me twenty-two years of marriage to recognize the extreme, faith-building value of long-term, ongoing, enthusiastic prayer. Had I learned this earlier, it could have been a family theme with dramatic results.

MOTHERS IN THE BIBLE

- Obedient Mary
- Trusting Elizabeth
- Doubtful Sarah
- Believing Hannah
- Deceptive Rebekah
- Wise Lois
- Loyal Ruth
- Sinful Eve
- Cunning Jezebel

I (Mary) wish I'd set up a system called Stones of Remembrance. The idea came to me after reading the biblical story of the Israelites crossing the Jordan River into the promised land. God had performed another miracle for them, stopping the flow of the river so they could cross on dry ground.

Once everyone was on the other side, the Lord told Joshua to choose twelve large stones from the center of the riverbed and have them carried to the river's edge. They were to pile them up there as a permanent reminder of what God had done for them. Then the Lord said, "In the future, when your children ask you, 'What do these stones mean?' tell them [the story of crossing the Jordan]. These stones are to be a memorial to the people of Israel forever" (Joshua 4:6–7).

My thought was to memorialize the significant happenings of our family by taking egg-sized stones and piling them in a basket on the floor. They would be unbreakable, big enough for children to handle, and more importantly, reminders of God's blessings. For example, when Marta broke her ankle and then healed up nicely, we could have written the words *broken ankle* on a stone, along with an appropriate Scripture reference and date.

Or when our budget was tight and God provided a bigger car, we could have put *minivan* on a stone. The stones would have prompted us to tell and retell the stories of God's goodness and of His involvement in our everyday lives, and we would have benefited from these visual reminders.

Whatever way you choose to characterize your family, start now while you still have little ones. By the time they're old enough to understand your theme, you will have established good family habits that are second nature to all of you.

A much-loved Sunday school chorus goes like this: "My God is so BIG, so strong, and so mighty; there's nothing my God cannot do." As children sing it, they shout the word "BIG" and believe it with all their hearts. We can take a lesson. Though we might have to lower our expectations of our children, we usually need to raise our expectations of God. It's true that there's nothing He can't do, yet we don't usually believe it. We mothers may not have all the answers to our parenting dilemmas, but God does, which is a powerful reason to go to Him regularly.

In the Psalms, God calls Himself a *rock of refuge* and invites us to come to His secure place of safety whenever we want. *Continually* and *always* are the words He uses in Psalm 71:3 below.

Of all the things both of us wish we'd known at the beginning of motherhood, the most important one is to have realized right from the get-go that no matter what else we tackled in life, nothing would have as great an impact or as far-reaching an influence as our mothering.

Consider the end before you begin.

> *Be my rock of refuge, to which I can always go;*
> *give the command to save me,*
> *for you are my rock and my fortress.*
> Psalm 71:3

What can you do today?

Write *Jesus* on a small rock and place it by your sink as a reminder of your parenting Partner.

We wish we'd known . . .

1. to choose a family mission statement as soon as we became parents.
2. to urge more Scripture memorization while our children were young.
3. that nothing could compare in importance to mothering the children God gave us.

Order Information

To order additional copies of this book, please visit
www.redemption-press.com.
Also available on Amazon.com and BarnesandNoble.com
Or by calling toll-free 1-844-2REDEEM.